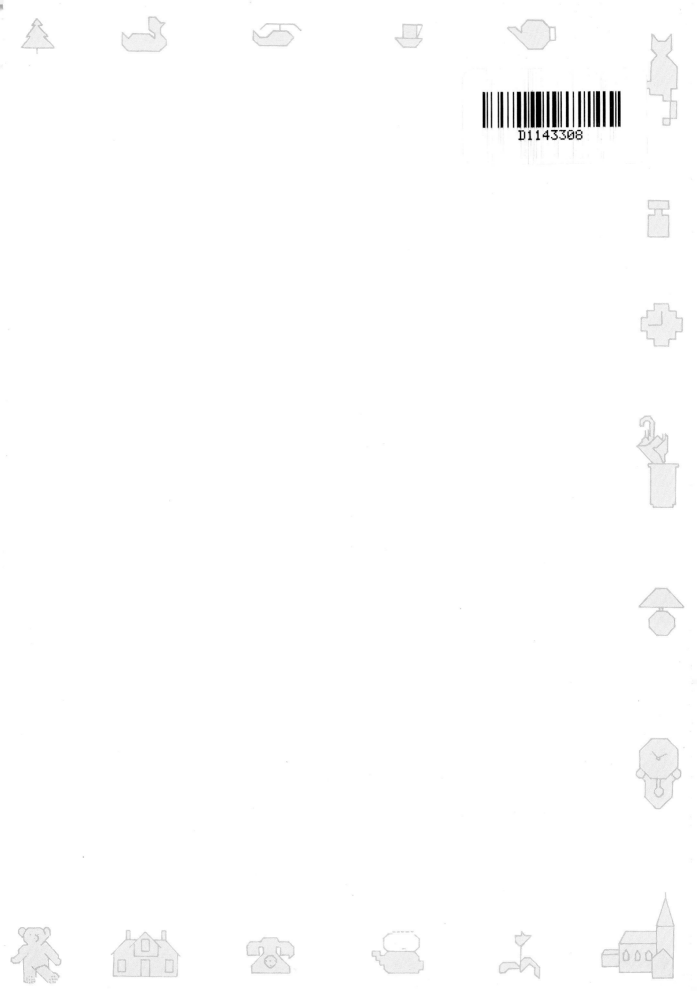

YOUR HOME
in
Cross Stitch

YOUR HOME
in
Cross Stitch

Barbara Thompson and Ann Green

David & Charles

A DAVID & CHARLES BOOK

© Barbara Thompson Designs, 1993

First published 1993

Barbara Thompson Designs have asserted their right to be identified
as author of this work in accordance with the Copyright,
Designs and Patents Act 1988.

A catalogue record for this book is available
from the British Library.

ISBN 0 7153 0001 6

Typeset by ABM Typographics Ltd Hull
and printed in England
by Butler & Tanner Ltd
for David & Charles
Brunel House   Newton Abbot   Devon

$\mathscr{C}$ONTENTS

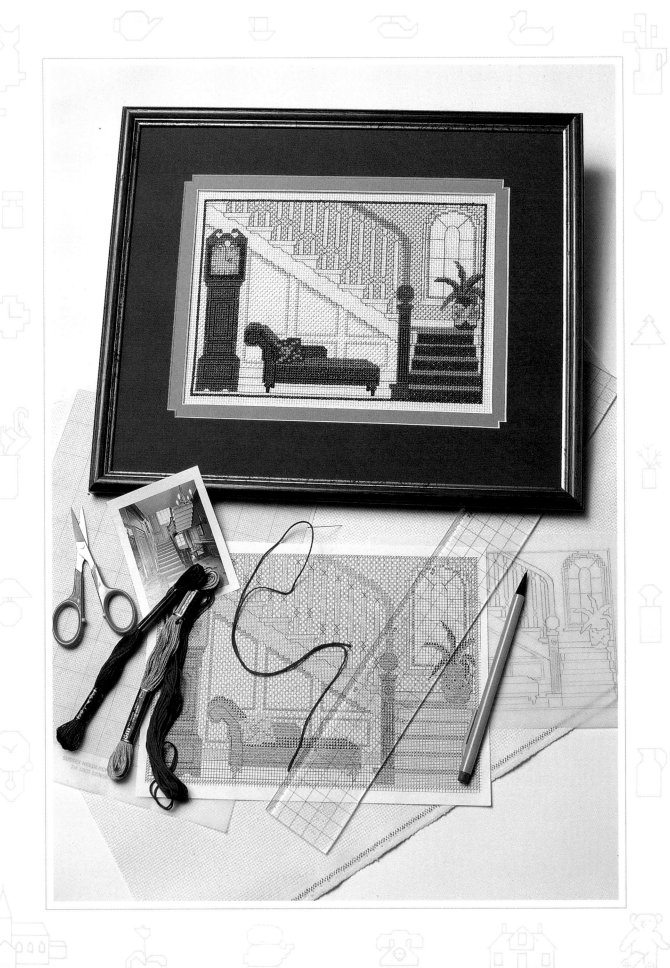

$\mathscr{I}$NTRODUCTION

'$\mathscr{H}$ome is where the heart is', and for embroiderers over the years, the home and everything connected with it has been a source of inspiration for traditional samplers, worked in cross stitch. For Barbara Thompson and Ann Green, the same inspiration has given rise first to a friendship, then a hobby, then a thriving business . . . and now this book.

It all began while both were at home, caring for young children. Barbara had started creating cross stitch pictures of friends' homes, after joining a local craft group. When Ann saw these, she immediately recognised their commercial potential and, although the two women lived 150 miles apart and neither had formal training either in art embroidery or in running a business, they formed a successful company, working cross stitch 'house portraits' to commission. From these beginnings, they have expanded to produce a range of counted cross stitch kits and designs that sell internationally, but that still take their inspiration from home.

Your Home in Cross Stitch provides all the information you will need, whether you are a beginner or an experienced stitcher, to create beautiful home portraits of your own. You will find basic techniques, step-by-step design instructions, complete charts with instructions on how to follow them, and individual motifs that will help you to portray your home and environment, inside and out. Whether you want to reproduce one of Barbara and Ann's designs, or simply take inspiration for your own home portrait, the information in this book will show you how.

The fact that Barbara and Ann are self-taught is an inspiration in itself. It is equally encouraging to know that you can achieve original, remarkable and beautiful results with the basic techniques explained here. Now, *your* home can be the starting point for *you*. You really do not need to know any more.

You simply need to stitch.

· 1 ·

$\mathscr{S}$TARTING $\mathscr{P}$OINTS

This chapter contains all the information you need to know to get started: which fabric to use, thread counts, using a frame, needles, thread, working cross stitch, diagonal half cross stitch, vertical or horizontal half cross stitch, back stitch, French knots, working from a chart and order of stitching.

FABRICS

Cross stitch is always worked on a fabric with an even weave. By this we mean a fabric where the warp (vertical) threads and weft (horizontal) threads are evenly spaced. These fabrics are available in linen or cotton, and by the yard (or metre) or in pre-cut pieces. All good embroidery or haberdashery centres and shops will sell this type of fabric. They will know what you are asking for and will be able to guide your choice. There are two main types of fabric to choose from: blockweave and evenweave.

BLOCKWEAVE

If you are a beginner, a good fabric to start on is Aida. This is a cotton material in which the threads are packed together during the weaving process in blocks with little holes in between. This gives the appearance of squares on the fabric which makes it easy to position and work the stitches. Each square will be the basis of one cross stitch (Fig 1A). Aida is reminiscent of the larger scale fabric, known as Binka, that we made into tray cloths and cushions in primary school!

Hardanger is a cotton fabric available in a wide range of colours. It is made up of pairs

of threads woven together to give a dense background, while still leaving easily seen holes between the warp and weft.

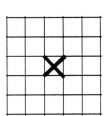

FIG 1A Cross stitch worked on Aida fabric

EVENWEAVE

This differs from Aida and Hardanger in that the warp and weft threads are not grouped or blocked, but are evenly spaced and close together, so that no holes show between the threads. Linda and Jobelan are examples of evenweave fabric. If the fabric is very fine, it can be difficult to count the threads. Stitches are worked over the threads on the fabric (Fig 1B).

STITCH COUNTS

How far apart the warp and weft are will determine the size of the stitch worked. Fabric for cross stitch is graded according to the stitch count, or number of blocks of threads there are to 1in (2.5cm). If the stitch count is high, the weave will be fine in texture and the size of each stitch worked will be smaller. A lower stitch count means that the weave is larger and the size of each stitch worked is larger too. For example, an 11 count fabric means that there are 11 blocks of thread and, therefore, up to 11 stitches to 1in (2.5cm). A 14 count fabric will accommodate 14 stitches to 1in (2.5cm) This means that for the 14 count fabric, slightly smaller stitches will be worked than for the 11 count fabric. An image worked on the 14 count fabric will have a finer look.

Evenweave and blockweave fabrics are available in a wide range of thread counts. You can choose from 11, 14, 16, 18, 22 and through to linen with a thread count of 27 or higher. If you are a beginner or have problems with your eyesight, choose a more open weave, or work each stitch across two strands at a time (Fig 1C).

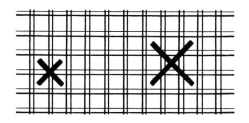

FIG 1B Cross stitch worked over one strand of warp and weft on evenweave fabric

FIG 1C Cross stitch worked over two strands of warp and weft on evenweave fabric

USING A FRAME

There is no right or wrong way to work cross stitch. It may traditionally have been worked on a frame but this is not strictly necessary, because the even tension of cross stitch means that the fabric does not become distorted. If working without a frame, take care to work with a firm, even tension, but do not pull the thread so tight as to enlarge the holes

in the fabric. Working with other stitches *can* distort the fabric, making a frame essential.

If you do choose to use a frame, either a hoop or a rectangular embroidery frame can be used. If you are using a hoop, make sure that the whole area being worked fits within it. Moving the hoop over areas already worked can flatten or distort the stitches.

FABRIC EDGES

You will find when handling blockweave fabrics that they fray very little. To begin with however, you may wish to oversew the fabric edges or bind them with masking tape to prevent any fraying. If you use a rectangular frame, hem the fabric to stop it fraying when you lace it into the frame.

TAPESTRY NEEDLES

Tapestry needles differ from usual sewing needles in that they have a fairly large 'eye', to take multiple strands of embroidery thread, and a comparatively rounded 'point' to slide through the hole in the fabric rather than puncturing the material.

The thickness of the needle is indicated by a number. The higher the number, the finer the needle. For cross stitch, it is best to use a fairly fine needle, size 24 or 26.

THREAD

Cross stitch can of course be done on canvas with wool, but in this book we are assuming you will use cotton threads on cotton or linen fabric. The threads that are normally used are the six-stranded embroidery threads, often called 'silks'. They are, in fact, cotton. The strands are separated to give a finer effect (see overleaf).

The two leading brands of thread in the UK are Anchor and DMC. Colour references are given for both in the charts. We have not given numbers of skeins required for each project, as this varies according to the stitch count of your fabric.

As a more experienced stitcher you may wish to use silk or metallic threads to achieve special effects, and these are available from specialist suppliers.

USING METALLIC THREADS

There are many metallic threads on the market and you must experiment to find one that suits you. Some 'shard' or unravel as you pull the thread through the fabric, because the metallic covering peels off from the nylon underneath. The one we find easiest to use is Effektgarn from Coats Anchor. It is extremely fine, so we use three strands in the needle as we stitch. There are others, mainly Japanese, which are readily available in specialist craft shops. These are expensive, but very effective used in small quantities.

SEPARATING STRANDS

As explained above, the stitch count of the fabric will determine the size of your cross and that will influence the number of strands used. The larger the stitch the greater the number of strands of thread that will be needed.

Fabric (stitches per inch)	Cross Stitch	Outline
Aida 11	3	2
Aida 14	2	1
Aida 18	1	1
Hardanger 22	1	1
Linda 27 (over 2 strands)	2	1
Linen 32 (over 2 strands)	2	1

Number of thread strands to use

Use the table as a guide to help you decide how many strands of thread you will use for cross stitch and back stitch on your chosen fabric. For example, a beginner using 14 count Aida will stitch with just two strands

of her chosen thread. Cut off a stitching length of about 60cm (24in) and separate two strands from the six. This is most easily done by pulling out one strand at a time. In this way the thread is less likely to tangle.

WORKING CROSS STITCH

To sew a single cross stitch bring the needle up through the material at the bottom left of where the stitch is to be. Cross diagonally over one block and insert the needle down through the top right corner. Now bring the needle up through the material in the bottom right, and cross over diagonally to put the needle down through the top left of the block (Fig 2).

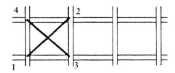

FIG 2 How to work a single cross stitch

If you count the needle 'strokes' you will notice that the needle always comes up through the material on odd numbers and goes down through the material on even numbers.

To sew a row of several cross stitches adjacent to each other, starting from the left bring the needle up through the bottom left of the first stitch and down through the top right to create the first half of the stitch, then repeat this for the next stitch (Fig 3A)

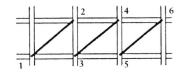

FIG 3A Working a row of cross stitch

When you have completed the required number of stitches in a row come back along the row completing the second part of each stitch, bringing the needle up through the bottom right and back down through the top left (Fig 3B).

There is really only one wrong way to stitch, and that is to work some cross stitches with the top stitch pointing one way and then others with the top stitch pointing the other way. The effect is uneven and untidy. If you follow the instructions above, you won't make this mistake.

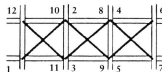

FIG 3B Completing a row of cross stitch

DIAGONAL HALF CROSS STITCH (THREE-QUARTER CROSS STITCH)

To achieve finer detail, for example on curved edges, it is possible to cover half the square only. One part of the stitch is formed by bringing the needle up through one corner of the square and putting it down through the centre of the square. The other part of the stitch is then formed in the normal way, by crossing from corner to corner (Fig 4).

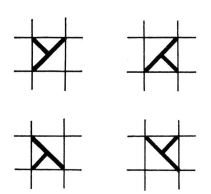

FIG 4 Diagonal half cross stitch (three-quarter cross stitch)

VERTICAL OR HORIZONTAL HALF CROSS STITCH

Again, this may be used to achieve a finer effect by forming a whole cross, but one which covers either the vertical or horizontal half of the square only (Fig 5).

FIG 5A Vertical half cross stitch   *FIG 5B Horizontal half cross stitch*

BACK STITCH

The only other stitch you will use in conjunction with cross stitch is back stitch. This is

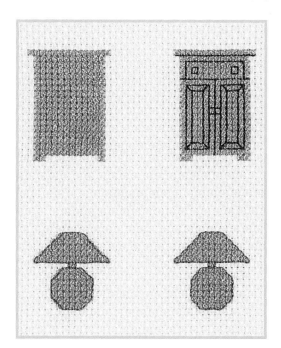

Back stitch can be used to pick out detail, as on the cabinet. When outlining, be aware of the effect you are creating. Compare the untidy result on the lamp (left) with that of sympathetic outlining (right)

used selectively to clarify fine detail and give an outline (Fig 6).

Bring the needle up at 2 then down at 1.

Next bring the needle up at 3 and down at 2.

Continue in this way; up at 4 down at 3, up at 5 down at 4 and so on.

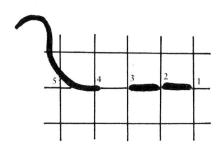

FIG 6 How to work back stitch

Back stitch can only be worked after the cross stitch, since it is worked on top of the stitches.

When the back stitch needs to go round the outside edge of the cross stitching, guide the thread with your thumb as you stitch to push the back stitch firmly to the outside edge rather than working it on top of the stitches. We call this 'sympathetic' outlining (see photograph on page 11).

FRENCH KNOTS

These are suitable for dots such as the eyes of the teddy bear in Nursery Items on page 103.

To work a French knot, right handed, bring the needle up through the fabric just one warp thread to the right of where you want the knot to be (this may be in the centre of a square if using blockweave material).

Holding the thread firmly with the left hand, place the needle point close to where the thread comes up out of the fabric and twist the thread twice round the needle. Securing the twists with the left thumb, push the needle down through the fabric one warp thread to the left of where the needle came up originally. Still holding the left thumb in place, pull the thread gently down through

the fabric until only the 'knot' remains on the surface.

Left-handed stitchers should reverse the left and right hand instructions.

WORKING FROM A CHART

Many cross stitch projects involve following a chart. This is presented in the form of a diagram drawn on graph paper. As the fabric you work is thought of as being divided into squares, it is easy to see that your job is to work stitches onto the squares on the fabric so that they correspond to the marked squares on the graph-paper chart. The suggested colours are shown by symbols, rather as in a painting-by-numbers design. If you can look at the symbols on the chart and work stitches in the corresponding colours in the right place on the fabric, then you can work any of the designs in this book and any you create yourself (see chart 1).

INSTRUCTIONS FOR SPIKY TOP CONSERVATORY

The design measures 70 squares by 50 squares.

Cross stitch
Using two strands of thread, work all cross stitches as follows: a) //// then b) XXXX so that the top stitches all point the same way (see Figs 3A and B).

Half cross stitch
If the colour symbol appears in the corner of a square rather than in the centre, work a half cross stitch in that diagonal half of the square (see Fig 4).

Back stitch
Finally, work the outlines shown on the chart in back stitch (see Fig 6 and photograph on page 11).

CHART 1 Spiky Top Conservatory

COLOUR KEY

		Anchor	DMC
—	Grey	400	317
▲	Dark green	879	500
U	Medium green	244	701
●	Light green	241	704
X	Brown	351	400
O	Pink	895	223
T	Wine	70	915

Outlines
Conservatory top   Grey (400, 317)
Plain lines of birdcage   Brown (351, 400)
Patterned lines of birdcage, floor   Grey (400, 317)
Left and centre plants   Wine (70, 915)
Right plant   Dark green (879, 500)

Stitched Spiky Top Conservatory

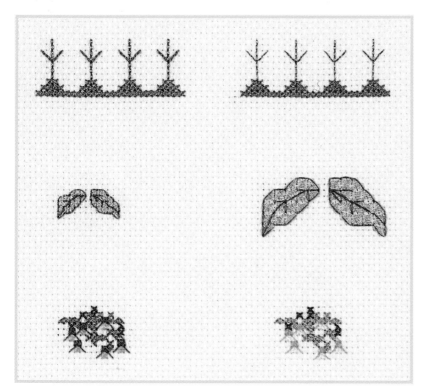

The bold spikes on top of the conservatory, worked first with two strands (left), and then one

The same leaf shown stitched to two different sizes to show outlining and the effect of scale clearly

The colour keys provided with the charts are only intended as a guide. Here the standard fuchsia has been stitched in two different colourways. Don't be afraid to experiment with the colours of your choice

The first step is to find the centre of the design on the chart, and then the centre of your fabric.

For the fabric, simply fold it in half, and then in half again, to pinpoint the centre (Fig 7).

FIG 7 *Finding the centre of a piece of fabric*

Mark the centre of each side of the chart, and then follow the marks to the middle to find the centre point. This is a good enough approximation; tedious counting of squares is not required.

It is a good idea at this stage to mark the centre of the fabric by making a stitch with coloured thread at the centre point on each of the four sides (Fig 8). This will ensure that the picture sits squarely on the fabric, leaving an equal border on all four sides. In our example you can see that the stem of the standard fuchsia plant is an obvious centre.

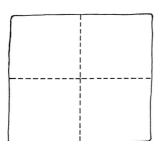

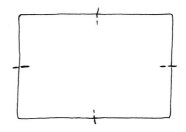

FIG 8 *Marking the sides of a piece of fabric*

Each symbol on the chart represents a colour. For example, ▲ equals dark green; O equals pink. In each square in which the symbol ▲ appears you will place a cross in dark green. Similarly, whenever a O appears you will stitch in pink. The two brands of embroidery thread we list in this book are Anchor and DMC, which are available worldwide. As the shade numbers are not an exact match, it is best not to mix them in one design.

Once a start has been made, the cross stitches will simply follow on outwards from the centre in whichever direction you are working and should be in the right place. This is where you will need to count! Check the chart, count the symbols, and work the correct number of cross stitches in the colour indicated in the colour key provided. In our example, for instance, X equals brown, therefore five X's equals five brown cross stitches. Simple, isn't it?

Of course, you need not feel restricted by these shade lists, and you will be able to substitute your own preferences as you become more confident.

This design, stitched on a 14 count Aida, would be best worked in two strands for the cross stitch and a single strand for the back stitch. It is still possible, however, to exercise your own taste in some matters. For example, the general rule is to use one strand of thread for all outlining on a 14 count Aida, but although we feel the delicate plants are best outlined this way, the bold spikes on the top of the structure could be worked using either one strand or two (see photograph on page 15). The choice is yours.

ORDER OF STITCHING

The dot in Fig 9 marks the centre of the chart. Two squares below this is the top of the fuchsia stem. This would be an appropriate place to start (a).

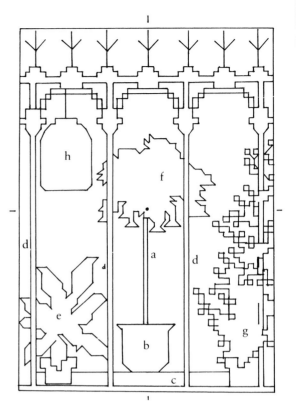

FIG 9 *Order of stitching for the Spiky Top Conservatory*

Having completed the stem, next stitch the pot (b).

The base would be the next logical place to stitch (c). This will need careful counting: count from under the pot to the right-hand end of the base and then stitch back to the left-hand edge. Simply repeat this for the three lines deep shown on the chart.

You can now build up the conservatory structure, as the base of each stanchion leads directly out of the base (d).

The plants can be stitched in any sequence you like as each has a 'guide' in the building structure (e, f, g).

Finally, stitch in the birdcage (h).

Once all the cross stitch has been completed, work the outlines in back stitch.

· 2 ·

GARDEN PLOTS

*Gardens make ideal subjects for cross stitch pictures. There
are so many interesting shapes and appealing colours to use,
and you certainly don't need to be a gardener to appreciate
them. Once you start looking at garden scenes with the eye of a
cross stitcher, you will see that the possibilities are endless.
And with such inspiration literally right outside your door, you
can start working on a garden picture whenever the mood
takes you.*

Of course, there are certain technical problems involved in designing and stitching a convincing and pleasing garden scene, and these might not be immediately obvious to a beginner at cross stitch. But that is precisely why we have chosen gardens as a starting point for designing your own cross stitch picture. If you read the instructions on planning, perspective and colour, and see how we have integrated these different elements into the Large Formal Garden project (see pages 18–21), you will see how all these elements can be applied to your own design. Together with other charts in this chapter, it should tell you most of what you need to know to start producing your own pictures with confidence.

MATERIALS

To start drawing your own designs, you will need a sharp, soft pencil, an eraser and some sheets of graph paper. Standard graph paper is available in different grid sizes or squares to 1in (2.5cm), and it is easiest to work with one that has squares approximately the same size as the squares on your evenweave fabric. This makes copying and/or tracing and transferring your designs onto graph paper much simpler, as the finished size of your chart will be the same as the finished size of your stitched picture and you will not need to think about scaling up or down.

Transparent graph paper is also available through good needlecraft shops or quality stationers. This allows you to trace straight onto the graph paper. It also comes in different grid sizes.

If you cannot find transparent graph paper then try placing a piece of ordinary graph paper over the top of the photograph or picture, paper clip the two together securely and then hold them against a window or over a glass top table with a light underneath. With the light shining through it, this system works nearly as well as transparent graph paper.

LARGE FROM SMALL

Should you wish to try designing a large garden scene as we have done, you will be faced with the choice of what to include to achieve the best effect in terms of both design and sewing. Barbara gave a lot of thought to what she would like in this garden scene. You could include favourite features from your own garden or from gardens of friends and neighbours that have impressed you. Photographs of course are ideal; magazines or garden catalogues can provide useful reference material and sometimes clear pictures that you can trace.

(continued on p24)

INSTRUCTIONS FOR LARGE FORMAL GARDEN

The design measures 200 squares by 150 squares, and the centre of each edge of the picture is marked on the chart. It is usual to start sewing this type of design from the centre but in this case you may prefer to start with the border, using your centre markings to ensure correct positioning.

Cross stitch
Using two strands of thread work all cross stitches as follows a) / / / / / b) XXXXX so that the top stitches all point the same way (see Figs 3A and B).

Half cross stitch
If the colour symbol appears in the corner of a square rather than in the centre, this indicates that you should do a half cross stitch in that diagonal half of the square (see Fig 4).

Back stitch
Finally, work the outlines shown on the Chart in back stitch. Use one strand of thread only for all back stitch.

Stitched Large Formal Garden. Notice how varying the texture of stitching creates contrast and movement

CHART 2
Large Formal Garden

COLOUR KEY

		Anchor	*DMC*
/	Dark green	879	500
▲	Medium green	244	701
S	Light yellow/ green	241	704
I	Light blue/ green	208	563
X	Dark brown	381	838
●	Stone	393	640
ℓ	Sandstone	373	437
—	Off white	830	3033
+	Light grey	399	415
(	Dark grey	400	317
O	White	01	White
U	Yellow	300	745
▽	Brick	5975	356
<	Light blue	130	799
T	Dark blue	137	798
∧	Palest blue	975	3753
■	Purple	102	550
\	Mauve	109	210
□	Dark peach	9575	353
ʘ	Light peach	4146	3774
♦	Pink	76	603

Outlines

Conservatory, summerhouse wheelbarrow	Dark grey (400, 317)
Conservatory plants, iris leaves	Dark green (879, 500)
Delphinium stems	Light yellow/ green (241, 704)
Delphinium leaves	Medium green (244, 701)
All stonework	Dark brown (381, 838)
Iris flowers	Purple (102, 550)

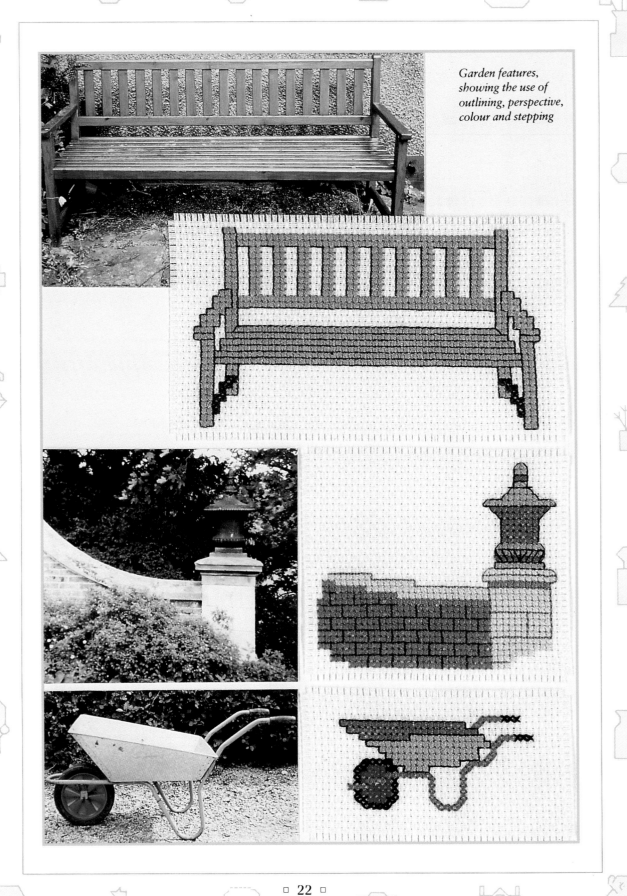

Garden features, showing the use of outlining, perspective, colour and stepping

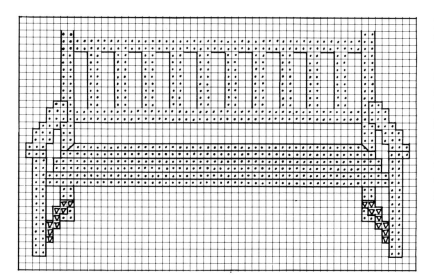

INSTRUCTIONS FOR GARDEN FEATURES

CHART 3
On this bench, outlining is used to show the planks of wood. We outlined the back and one side only, to emphasise the three-dimensional effect (see photograph opposite)

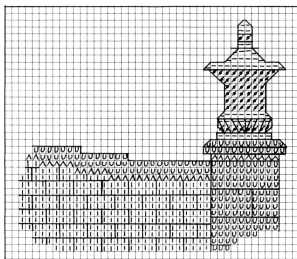

CHART 4 (left)
The use of two shades of grey, light and dark, gives the effect of light falling on the metal of this garden urn (see photograph opposite)

CHART 5 (bottom left)
The only way of showing the diagonal line of this wheelbarrow on the chart is to step it. The stitched version looks much less angular (see photograph opposite)

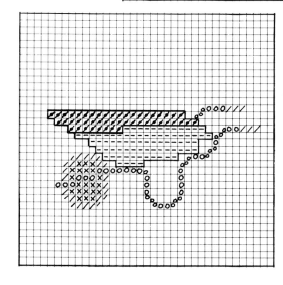

COLOUR KEY

		Anchor	DMC
●	Dark grey	400	317
—	Light grey	399	415
O	Medium green	244	701
/	Black	403	310
X	Red	9046	321
●	Sandstone	373	437
▽	Dark brown	381	838
U	Off white	830	3033
I	Brick	5975	356
∧	Stone	393	640

Outlines

Wheelbarrow and urn	Black (403, 310)
Bench, bricks	Dark brown (381, 838)
Stonework	Stone (393, 640)

BE SELECTIVE

To give an impression of your own garden you don't need to show the whole scene, just a part of it will do. Take a bench, for example, which you have in a sunny spot, put a wheelbarrow nearby and perhaps fill the barrow with plants. Then dot a few plants around and you have a complete picture which people will recognise as your garden because it contains perhaps just one key element.

SKETCH AND PHOTOGRAPH

Sketch if you can, photograph if you prefer. Bear in mind when you photograph that it is difficult to graph diagonal lines, the horizontal and the vertical are always simpler, so when you photograph be 'straight on' to the object. To snap a bench for instance, position yourself centrally and crouch down to its level. This will give good vertical and horizontal lines (see photographs on page 22).

Similarly, with a wheelbarrow there are obviously going to be some diagonals, but if photographed straight on at its own height you will have the best angles for cross stitch.

DRAWING UP THE CHART

The next step is to transfer your designs onto graph paper. Copy or trace from your sketch or photograph, drawing the outlines and

shapes directly onto the sheet of graph paper using a soft pencil. You will then need to convert these outlines and details into a stitchable chart, using the 'stepping' and 'squaring off' techniques described below.

STEPPING

When transferring your design to the graph paper it is not possible to mark diagonal lines; it has to be stepped. You may feel you have lost the line of the object and that it looks awkward, but once stitched, and especially if outlined, the eye does not notice the steps (see Fig 10).

SQUARING-OFF

If you are tracing or copying pictures to add to your cross stitch design, you will certainly be faced with the problem of squaring-off sooner or later. This means that any curved lines will have to be angled to form squares on the graph paper so that you can work them in cross stitch (see Figs 11A and B). This will make the shape look more stylised, but if you are working on a fairly fine stitch count the results will be excellent. Another possibility is to use some half cross stitches in the design to help retain the details of the shape (see Figs 12A and B).

PLAN

In our design, the choice of a large Victorian-style conservatory placed in the front left-

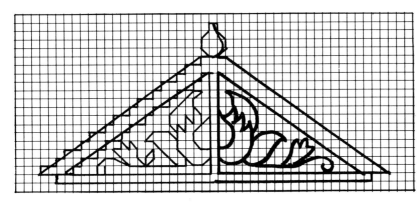

FIG 10 Charting roof shapes from a sketch or tracing using the techniques of stepping and squaring off (see photographs on page 27)

hand corner was the starting point. We wanted another building, so included the little gazebo. This had to be placed further back and reduced in size to give the correct perspective. The third architectural structure, the archway and bridge, was placed right at the back so that the impression given was of three terraced levels. These also had to be reduced in size to continue the perspective.

PERSPECTIVE

When designing and working a cross stitch picture, you can create an impression of depth by introducing perspective. The design techniques described above should help. Steps are a good perspective device. In our design they reduce in width quite noticeably from the bottom step to the top.

The best way to achieve this is to take a photograph of a set of steps and follow it. You will see clearly how they spread right out towards the front. Any well-illustrated gardening book will include a photograph of a handsome set of steps, possibly with urns at the top or bottom, or both, that you could copy or trace for your design.

TREES AND FLOWERS

Once the main pieces of architecture are positioned on the chart and the ground levels

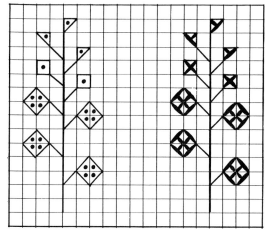

FIG 12A Diagonal half cross stitch is shown on the chart with a symbol in just half the square

FIG 12B The half cross stitch is worked in the part of the square indicated to give a fine, detailed effect

are established, you will need to think about plants.

For the trees, again look at pictures in books to get the general outline shapes, then draw just the outlines on the chart.

In the foreground, some structural details of the flowers should be visible, so choose plants that have a distinctive shape. We chose irises, and first of all drew the shape of the iris flower on to the graph paper, then squared it off (Figs 11A and B). Plants in the background need not be shown in such detail. You will probably rely more on colour to suggest the various shapes and forms.

COLOUR MATCH

Where there are tumbling masses of flowers to be represented then it is fun to experiment with colour: just select shades you favour and put them together randomly. For foliage and grass, choose plenty of different greens and scatter your selection over the paper to fill in the spaces.

When choosing colours for trees, try using dark shades to show the underparts of branches which will usually be in shadow, then lighter green for the sunlit, upper surfaces.

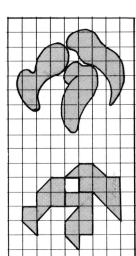

FIG 11A The distinctive, curving shape of the iris flower is not suitable for working in cross stitch

FIG 11B Squaring off the shape on graph paper makes it possible to work the design in full cross stitch and diagonal half cross stitch

Stitched Mahogany Conservatory. Showing some plants through the 'glass' creates a feeling of depth. The chart and instructions for this design are on pages 28-9

SPACE AND TEXTURE

Never be afraid to leave spaces, this is one of the ways your picture will achieve a varied texture. For instance, if the windows in the conservatory and the gazebo were filled with stitches, there would be no feeling of depth.

Similarly, when showing a close-up view of a tree, don't be afraid to leave unstitched spaces as this will give the impression of light shining through the branches, and of individual leaves. The spaces will show the light, delicate nature of the tree, and although you will obviously not stitch each individual leaf,

the impression will be very realistic.

Another device you can use to vary the texture of your design is to work alternate cross stitch. This is, as it sounds, simply a matter of stitching every other square with a cross stitch; so work a stitch, miss a stitch and so on across the row. On the next row fill in the alternate square to the one in the preceding row. The effect produced is less dense than when every square is filled. Compare the gravel path in the Large Formal Garden design with the surface of the wall. This is one way you can show differences in the texture of building materials.

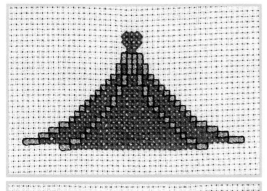

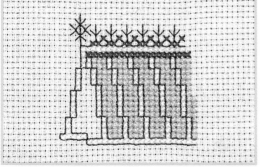

GARDEN STRUCTURES

(Left) *Two interesting roof shapes typical of gazebos and conservatories. Both show how to achieve curved or diagonal surfaces by 'stepping' the outline*

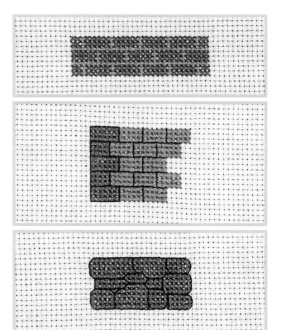

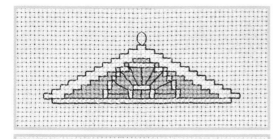

(Above) *a) A brick wall shown with mortar in cross stitch*
b) Cornerstones shown neatly in a different colour from the rest of the wall
c) A stone wall with mortar, shown this time in outline stitch only

(Left) *Three conservatory tops*
a) A gable end. The use of pale blue thread gives the impression of glass against whitewood. Outlining in dark grey is needed to show the patterns
b) The finials are picked out in dark grey outline with a single strand of thread. These are usually painted in white, but it is necessary to stitch them in grey to make them show up effectively
c) This shows the use of traditional stained glass colours and patterns, with dark grey outlining used to imitate leaded lights

GARDEN FEATURES

Try working the garden features on pp22-3 to help you develop a feel for perspective, colour and texture, and the uses of outlining.

You can work these as practice pieces on spare fabric, or incorporate them into a design of your own. Follow the stitch instructions for the Large Formal Garden.

GARDEN STRUCTURES

In the Large Formal Garden design, the garden structures really help to hold the picture together. Their solid forms and straight lines are the perfect foil for the softer details of plants and trees. Practising on these small buildings will help when you come to try house portraits, too. You can perfect your technique and try out different effects for building materials on a small scale.

Colour is far more important in buildings than you might at first imagine. Just look at a number of brick structures and you will see just how varied the colours can be, with yellows, beige, bright terracotta or brownish red. But don't waste time trying to find exactly the same shade of thread – always use a brighter shade than that of the real building material. Similarly with stonework, a brighter shade will always look better in the finished embroidery.

For red brick, for example, choose a nice bright, brick red. For sandstone, try a bright yellow-brown, or two contrasting stone shades. Work the cornerstones in one shade of brown and the rest of the stone in another. To give the impression of rough stone, use just one colour for the stone then outline over the top (see photograph on page 27). This is discussed further in Chapter 3.

MAHOGANY CONSERVATORY

This design was directly inspired by a friend's conservatory. The base has been featured in brick but could just as easily be in stone.

Hardwood conservatories are popular, but it would be no problem to show this as a white-painted structure. The effect of the background colour should be considered. We have used ivory Aida and the brown shows up against it nicely. If you chose white for the conservatory, then you could either outline in a darker shade, perhaps charcoal grey, or choose a darker background fabric. A wide range of fabric colours are available, white, blues, reds and greens, to black.

In this design we have used many half cross stitches to achieve the fine detail of the plants. Do not be afraid of half cross stitch: it requires slightly more concentration but gives a distinctive, fine look, especially when outlined with care (Fig 4 and 6, pp11 and 12).

INSTRUCTIONS FOR
MAHOGANY CONSERVATORY

The design measures 70 squares by 50 squares, and the centre of each edge of the picture is marked on the chart. It is usual to start sewing this type of design from the centre but in this case you may prefer to start with the border, using your centre markings to ensure correct positioning

Cross stitch
Using two strands of thread work all cross stitches as follows a) ///// b) XXXXX so that the top stitches all point the same way (Figs 3A and B).

Half cross stitch
If the colour symbol appears in the corner of a square rather than in the centre, this indicates that you should do a half cross stitch in that diagonal half of the square (see Fig 4).

Back stitch
Finally, work the outlines shown on the chart in back stitch. Use one strand of thread only for all back stitch.

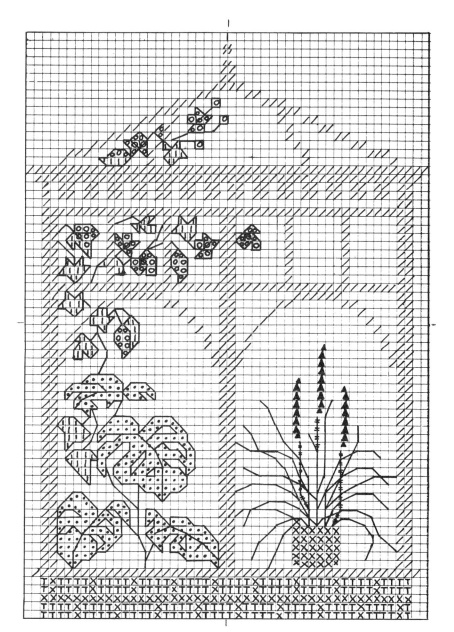

CHART 6 Mahogany Conservatory

COLOUR KEY

		Anchor	DMC
T	Terracotta	340	919
/	Brown	351	400
●	Medium green	244	701
▲	Pink	9575	353
X	Grey	399	415
I	Dark green	879	500
O	Light green	208	563

Outlines

Roof spike	Brown (351,400)
Plant stems, veins and leaf outlines	Dark green (879,500)
Flower stalks	Light green (208,563)

SUMMERHOUSE

This summerhouse was made by one of our friends in her own garden from bits of an old shed.

Its unusual shape inspired us to make a picture of it. We started by taking a photograph, then traced it by paper clipping the photograph behind the graph paper and holding it against a window so that the light shone through. The shape of the outline and the windows was perfectly clear. The details were filled in afterwards.

There were no flowers around the summerhouse, and that would have made a rather plain picture, so we applied poetic licence, dotting the flowers in a pleasing arrangement so as to make a full and interesting image.

Stitched Summerhouse. We invented a pleasing display of plants in front of this structure to soften the lines and add interest

INSTRUCTIONS FOR SUMMERHOUSE

The design measures 56 squares by 65 squares. Follow stitch instructions for the Large Formal Garden, page 18.

COLOUR KEY

		Anchor	DMC
O	Grey green	876	502
—	Dark green	879	500
▲	Medium green	244	701
V	Light green	208	563
/	Olive green	846	936
·	Light brown	378	407
X	Off white	830	3033
S	Yellow	307	783
T	Pink	76	603
U	Mauve	109	210

Outlines

Roof, door panels	Dark brown (381, 838)
Windows, window sill paving, door handle	Dark grey (400, 317)
Plants	Medium green (244, 701)

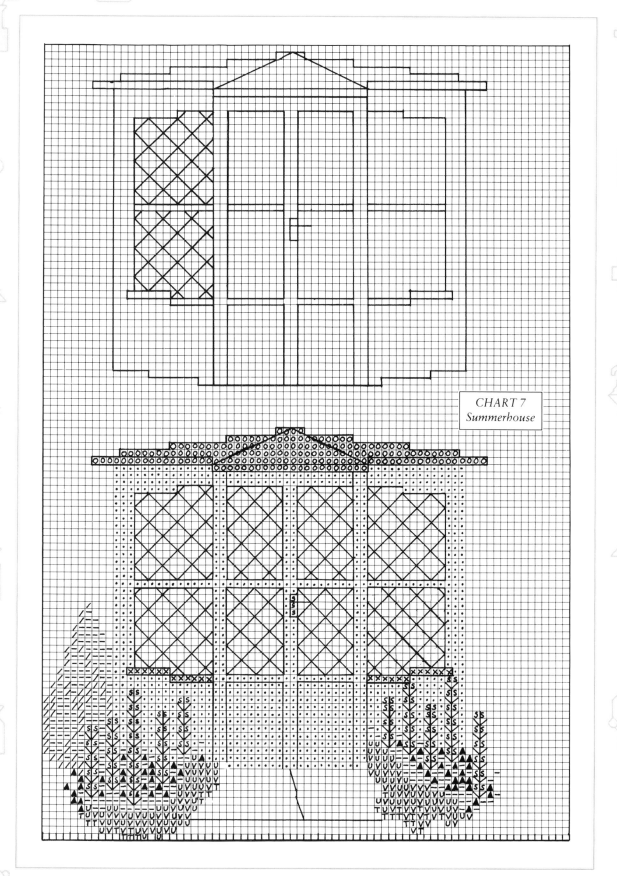

CHART 7
Summerhouse

3

BUILDING BLOCKS

*Once you progress to showing a whole house, you will realise
that there are a great many decisions to make before you work
the first stitch. Spend as long as you can just looking at your
subject, and try sketching parts of it in detail to make you more
aware of the range of textures and colours. Then it's back to
the drawing board!*

BUILDING TEXTURES

There are any number of ways of showing
brick and stone, and we discussed some of
them briefly in Chapter 2. The key principle
is to look carefully at the colours of a building, and choose brighter shades. When looking at a house you will notice it consists
mainly of the walls, which may be brick or
stone; the roof, which may be slate or tiles;
and the woodwork, which may be any colour. You will want to feature these elements
in your design in a way that both captures the
character of the house and creates a pleasing
picture.

COLOUR BRIGHT

Having studied the main features of the
house, put together a group of threads in colours which are similar to but brighter than
the ones you have observed, and which also
tone together well. If you wish to represent a
greeny-grey or a bluey-grey tile roof, then try
to bring out the green or blue tones, rather
than going straight for grey. Then choose a
colour for the walls, which should be a
slightly brighter version of the real colour

but must also tone well with the choice you
have already made for the roof.

Paintwork will be next. It may be plain
white, but which white will go best with your
other two choices? Once you really start
observing colours you will become far more
sensitive to the infinite variations. Play
around with the colours until you achieve a
pleasing group: it really doesn't matter if you
no longer feel it is an accurate reproduction
of the house, what you are trying to create is
a picture *based* on the house.

STITCH MIX

There are also different ways of using cross
stitch to show variety in the surface textures
of a building. Crosses can be stitched in solid
rows, or by alternating the stitches, as
explained in Chapter 2. Stonework and brick
can be uniform in colour, but are also sometimes very uneven with different shades of
grey or brown, so be prepared to mix colours
if necessary. Do this by working alternate
stitches in two different shades, or by ming-
ling two or more colours randomly over the
whole area of stonework. Examples can be
seen on page 34.

OUTLINING

Outlining with back stitch, as explained in Chapters 1 and 2, will give you another technique to represent texture. If there are fancy shaped tiles on the roof, for example, draw them onto squared paper first to find the outline shape that you need. One of the most effective uses of outlining is on woodwork, to show panelling on doors or to pick out window panes. It is also very useful for wrought-ironwork; in fact, it would be hard to show this any other way. Thin, outline back stitches in black, even though the wrought-iron itself may be grey, will show up clearly.

STAINED GLASS

There are certain colours that are very characteristic of stained glass: a transparent green shade and a transparent blue shade, for example, are very common, so they are good to include as background colours. Pinks and wines are useful too.

The colours should provide contrast, but must remain subtle. Remember, they are usually seen with light shining through the glass, so the colours should be gently diffused – don't choose very bright shades. Outlining each area of colour with dark grey creates the effect of the lead glazing strips, and makes the whole picture more realistic.

BRICK AND STONEWORK

The photographs on page 34 show four examples of different ways we use to show bricks: brickwork with mortar visible; brickwork with pointing shown as an outline; brickwork shown as at a distance using alternate cross stitch; and Victorian brickwork with patterning of different coloured brick. Quite often this last type of brickwork is found as a frieze along the top of a building, or as fancy work just above a window.

We talked earlier, in Chapter 2, of the different effects that can be used to represent stonework. Some of these are shown and described on page 34.

ROOF TILES

The photographs overleaf show two examples of roof tiles and ridge tiles. You can make a striking feature by picking out the ridge tiles on a roof in a contrasting colour. The photograph shows a slate roof which we have worked in green, contrasting well with the red of the ridge tiles. Note also a more traditional blue-coloured slate with a fancy pattern. The outline stitch shows how the pattern can be easily varied.

WOODWORK

Weatherboarding is usually white woodwork, used to face the brick, and is common in some areas. Brown wood panelling is frequently used on modern houses.

There are two examples of panelling in the photograph on page 35, one on a grand, six-panel front door and one on a more rustic garage door or gate. Here we have used a dark background colour and white as the outline. In general, it is advisable to use a darker colour for outline but if the background is very dark, as in this case, and the outline is white then the contrast is strong enough.

STITCHING BUILDING TEXTURES AND FEATURES

The stitched examples of building textures and features shown overleaf demonstrate the level of effect and detail which can be achieved through clever choice of stitch and thread colour.

Each stitched sample is described in detail, to help you reproduce it exactly or adapt it to suit your own design.

SAMPLER OF BUILDING SURFACES

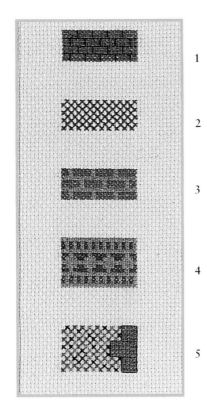

1 In this traditional pattern, the shape of the bricks is shown in outline, worked in black over cross stitch in terracotta. The brick size can be altered from 4x2 stitches as illustrated here, to 5, 6, or 7x3 stitches, as required

2 A more distant, general brick appearance can be achieved by using alternate cross stitch. This is useful for filling in walls, where other detail can be emphasised in complete cross stitch

3 A more detailed brick effect can be achieved by using a contrasting colour to show the mortar between the bricks

4 Many Victorian buildings are decorated by the use of two or more colours of brick worked into repeating patterns. Many variations are possible, but even the simplest combinations of two colours can produce very ornate and effective patterns

5 There are many ways of portraying general stonework, one of which is to use alternate stitch either in a single colour, or using a combination of two or more colours as shown here to provide a mottled, textured surface. More specific dressed stone can be stitched in complete cross stitch and outlined in a dark colour, in the same way that the cornerstones are shown here

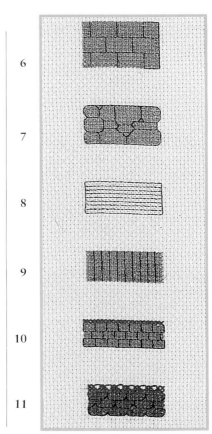

6 Classical stone buildings can be worked in complete cross stitch, with the outlines of each stone marked in back stitch in a dark colour

7 This example illustrates another way of showing rough stonework. The background is worked in one colour of a light tone and then the outlines are worked randomly in a dark tone to show uneven-sized stones. This is best achieved by drawing the outlines onto squared paper first

8 Weatherboarding on buildings is made up of planks running vertically or horizontally and this effect is achieved by stitching the background in the colour of the paint, as shown here, and then the horizontal planks outlined in dark grey or black

9 This example of vertical weatherboarding gives the impression of being unpainted wood and is worked as the previous example, but with the outlining worked vertically

10 Roof tiles and slates come in a wide variety of colours. This example shows a grey-green Lakeland slate, contrasting with terracotta ridge tiles. These are simple, small slates, with the pattern delineated in black outlining

11 A more ornate terracotta ridge-tile design is illustrated here, using a combination of a simple cross stitch pattern and a few lines of outline in the same colour. Contrasting with the terracotta, as is very common of Victorian and Edwardian buildings, we have used a blue-grey colour for the roof tiles, and worked a more ornate outline pattern in black back stitch

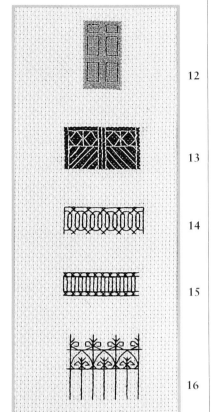

12

13

14

15

16

12 This example illustrates the way to tackle the stitching of a door, by filling in the whole door in cross stitch in a light shade, and working over this in back stitch in a dark shade to mark the panel outlines

13 Usually it is advisable to work outlines in a dark shade over a lighter cross stitch background. However, this example shows that it is sometimes possible to work light outlines over a dark background. White is the most effective colour to use in this technique, and patterns on large doors or fences can be shown in this way. Here the diagonal lines jump over several cross stitches at a time, so as not to be obscured by the background colour

14 Simple wrought-iron patterns, worked in a single strand of black thread, can give the impression of ornate and complicated designs. This example shows one possibility using mainly vertical lines, and is worked entirely in back stitch

15 This is a simplified version of a common iron railing design, using alternate cross stitches enclosed in horizontal lines at top and bottom. These rows are joined together by simple rows of vertical back stitch

16 This pattern is copied from an ornate iron railing design and is worked entirely in back stitch. These more complicated designs can be worked out on squared paper and, when repeated continuously, provide a very delicate contrast to the cross stitch in the rest of the picture

17 These are two examples of brackets seen in buildings such as conservatories, stations and colonnades, and are effective in adding ornate detail to a picture. They are worked in back stitch

18 Stained glass comes in many styles, and this example shows how to give the impression of a complicated, multi-coloured pattern. A limited number of pale colours is used and diagonal half stitches give the rounded appearance to the delicate leaf and flower shapes. Pale blue forms the background colour, with pale pink, yellow and green being used for the pattern. These colours are separated from each other by the use of dark grey outlining to mimic the lead

19 Here, panels of coloured glass form a border to the window and are separated from the main pane (shown in grey) by wooden glazing bars. This type of glass panelling is common in internal glass doors. This example is sewn in cross stitch

20 This example shows a different type of coloured glass border, where the main pane of glass is left blank and only the coloured border and the window frame are worked in cross stitch. Extra clarity is gained through outlining

21 Window glass shown from a distance, usually as part of a whole building, is generally effective if stitched in light grey. As this example shows, it is then possible to delineate window frames in cross stitch, and small glass panel outlines in a dark back stitch

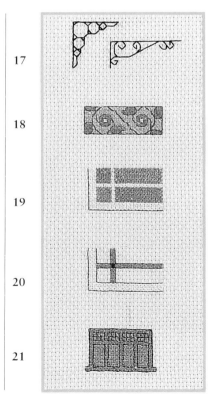

17

18

19

20

21

· 4 ·

ℋOUSE ℰXTERIORS

*The techniques we discussed in the previous chapters will come
in useful now. With the help of two examples, you can learn to
design, chart and stitch a portrait of your own house. The
examples are in the form of charts, each of which will make a
picture in itself should you wish. One is a smaller, simple house,
the other a larger, more elaborate Victorian home.*

YOUR OWN HOUSE PORTRAIT

If you are good at drawing, the first stage is to stand outside your own house and sketch. A far easier method is to take a photograph. This will ensure that the overall proportion, and the size of individual features in particular, are accurate. Remember to stand far enough back to take in the whole of the house but little or nothing of the surroundings, and try to place yourself squarely in the middle of the aspect you have chosen.

The colours don't matter at this stage. What is important is the outline shape and the placement of the various features, so a black and white photograph would do, or a colour one on a dull, wet day.

TRACING AND CHARTING

In Chapter 2 we described how to use plain or transparent graph paper to trace a design from a photograph. If your house photo is already the size that you would like your finished embroidery to be, (it is possible to have the picture enlarged to twice the normal

size, which may be perfect for 14 count), you can trace it straight on to graph paper in the way described on page 17. If not, you can scale it up onto the graph paper.

SCALING UP OR DOWN

Measure the photo of your house in fractions of an inch or millimetres. One square on the graph paper represents one unit. If you would like the image larger, then use two squares on the graph paper to one unit. Similarly, the image can be reduced by using one square on the graph paper to represent two units of measurement. Draw the outline of the house walls onto the graph paper first, then add the roof.

You will see from the sketch of the 1930s semi-detached house that, as we decided to 'detach' it for our purpose, the roof line is slightly different on each side (Fig 13A). In Fig 13B we have stepped the roof off at the side where it would have been joined to the neighbouring house. If you are dealing with a terraced house then the roof will need this treatment at both sides.

To do this, use a ruler to draw a diagonal

line in the desired place. Follow as closely to this line as possible, squaring off on the graph paper (see Fig 10, p24). The line is now 'stepped', which is the only possible way of showing any diagonal line in cross stitch.

Once you have drawn the outline on the graph paper, you should have some sort of rectangle with a roof shape on top. Then you can add the detail.

Measure the front door and place it in the correct position. Draw in the front door, draw in the windows, gables and chimneys, and gradually add any other smaller details. It is not necessary to colour in or mark each square in the colour chosen for the stitching at this stage. Only the outlines are needed for now (Fig 13B).

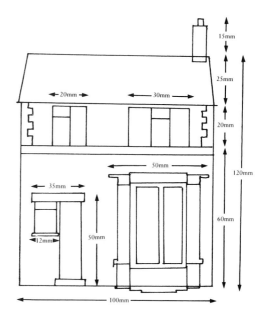

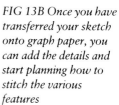

FIG 13A Measure your original sketch or tracing carefully, but keep the design as simple as possible

FIG 13B Once you have transferred your sketch onto graph paper, you can add the details and start planning how to stitch the various features

Stitched version of 1930s House. Bright colours and varied stitching patterns make a pleasing picture of this modest house, shown at the sketch stage in Figures 13A and B

INSTRUCTIONS FOR 1930s HOUSE

The design measures 136 squares by 100 squares. Follow stitch instructions for the Large Formal Garden, page 18.

Outlines

Brickwork	Brick (340, 919)
Window frames	White (01, White)
Door frame	Woodwork green (189, 943)

COLOUR KEY

		Anchor	DMC
—	Grey/green	876	502
/	Off white	830	3033
·	Brick	340	919
I	Light grey	399	415
∧	Dark grey	400	317
O	White	01	White
X	Light brown	373	437
U	Dark brown	381	838
▲	Woodwork green	189	943
▽	Plant green	244	701
S	Light blue	130	799
T	Dark blue	149	336

CHART 8 1930s House

ADDING DETAIL

Now you have a general plan for your house portrait, you can start to think about ways of stitching the component features so as to achieve the detail and contrast that make a picture interesting.

1930s HOUSE

You can see how a variety of effects was achieved with the 1930s semi-detached house that we drew and charted on graph paper as shown in Figs 13A and B.

ROOF-SLATE

This is a greenish grey with small smooth Lakeland slates. We have chosen to work every stitch of the roof, giving a smooth surface. As the slates are small and regular we decided not to outline individual slates.

PEBBLE DASH

This cream-washed pebble dash has a lovely rough surface which can be depicted by random placing of crosses in ones, twos and threes along each row. This random stitching contrasts well with the formal brickwork.

BRICK

The usefulness of alternate stitch was discussed in connection with the Large Formal Garden picture in Chapter 2. Here it is very effective for the brickwork, giving an impression of the neat, even rows of brick.

GLASS

In most types of cross stitch picture it is impossible to show objects through windows. The exceptions to this are the conservatory pictures with vast expanses of glass, but it would be far less effective here. If we try to show curtains they would detract from the lines of the window frame, rendering the external features of the house less distinct. As the object here is to show the exterior of the windows we simply fill in the windows with cross stitch.

WOODWORK

The colours chosen for the wood detail are intended to highlight these features. Decorative details, such as the woodwork along the top of the bay, are easily picked out by the colour contrast with their surroundings.

TWELVE STEPS TO SUCCESSFUL DESIGN

Provided you work systematically and follow these 12 basic steps, you should have no trouble producing your own house portrait.

1 Take the photo from straight on, aiming at the centre of the subject.

2 Choose graph paper with squares as near in size as possible to those on your fabric.

3 Draw an outline of the house onto your graph paper using one square to equal one unit of measurement, either a fraction of an inch or a millimetre on the photograph.

4 Scale the size up or down by doubling or halving the number of squares per unit.

5 Measure, then draw in windows, doors and other features to the same scale.

6 Adjust the slope of the roof.

7 Do the same for any other diagonal feature of the house.

8 Position any plants and trees in front of the house on the chart. These will need to be stitched first.

9 Decide on which cross stitch techniques to use for different building fabrics and textures. Try these out on a spare piece of material.

10 Choose all the colours and plot them on the chart.

11 Stitch the picture, working the cross stitch first and filling in the details with outlining.

12 Add other surrounding details, such as trees, the border or the name.

THE BURRS

DETAILS FROM THE BURRS

Although this house is much larger and has many more intricate details, it can be tackled in exactly the same way as the 1930s semi-detached. We first charted the whole house from a photograph. The most interesting part was choosing the best and most effective ways of using cross stitch to depict the various architectural details. Some of these details have been enlarged on page 43.

COLOUR KEY

		Anchor	DMC
O	Brick	340	919
X	Brown	381	838
·	Grey	399	415
—	White	01	White
/	Black	403	310
S	Stone	393	640

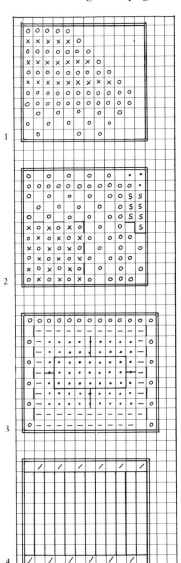

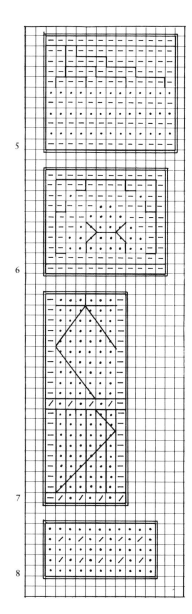

CHART 9 Details from The Burrs

Stitched version of The Burrs

(Opposite)
BURRS DETAIL
This sampler of enlarged details taken from 'The Burrs' shows you how architectural details can be represented using a variety of techniques

1 By selective use of a darker colour along with brick red it is possible to show shadow and texture in the ornate parapet. When viewed with the house as a whole, these alternate rows achieve a textured effect of raised rows of brickwork
2 Different brick patterns and textures are depicted here using the same combination of brick red and dark brown but in a different pattern, this time giving alternate diagonal rows. Other brick patterns are also shown here by a varied use of cross stitch and alternate cross stitch in the same colour
3 This window detail illustrates how best to use white outlines over grey cross stitch. Here the back stitch leaps over several cross stitches at a time to make the solid glazing bars stand out from the window glass
4 Whatever colour wrought-iron is painted in reality, it is shown most effectively if stitched in black or very dark grey. Here, very little cross stitch is used, the main effect coming from the use of back stitch

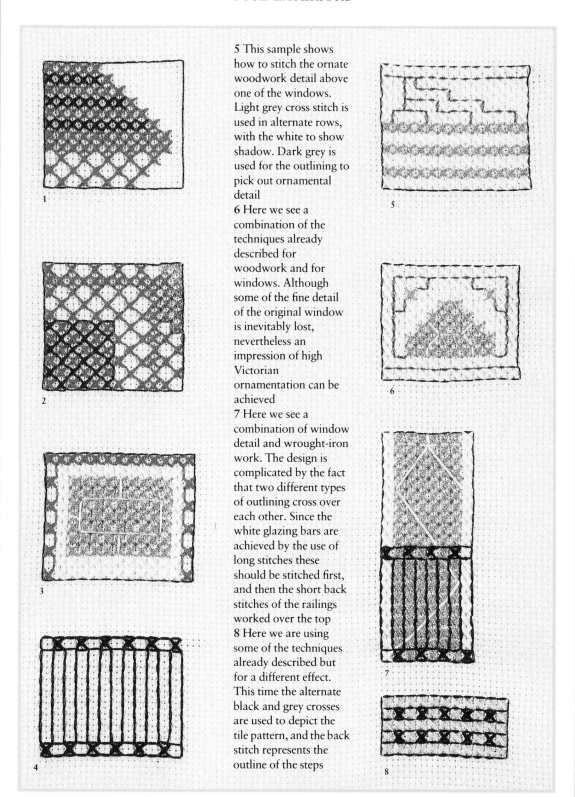

5 This sample shows how to stitch the ornate woodwork detail above one of the windows. Light grey cross stitch is used in alternate rows, with the white to show shadow. Dark grey is used for the outlining to pick out ornamental detail

6 Here we see a combination of the techniques already described for woodwork and for windows. Although some of the fine detail of the original window is inevitably lost, nevertheless an impression of high Victorian ornamentation can be achieved

7 Here we see a combination of window detail and wrought-iron work. The design is complicated by the fact that two different types of outlining cross over each other. Since the white glazing bars are achieved by the use of long stitches these should be stitched first, and then the short back stitches of the railings worked over the top

8 Here we are using some of the techniques already described but for a different effect. This time the alternate black and grey crosses are used to depict the tile pattern, and the back stitch represents the outline of the steps

Enlarged detail of stitching used for The Burrs

CHART 10 *The Burrs*

INSTRUCTIONS FOR THE BURRS

The design measures 224 squares by 96 squares.
Follow stitch instructions for the Large Formal
Garden, page 18.

COLOUR KEY

		Anchor	DMC
·	Brick	340	919
—	White	01	White
I	Stone	393	640
0	Medium grey	399	415
V	Pale grey	397	762
X	Black	403	310
/	Brown	381	838
\	Green	208	563

Outlines

Brickwork	Brick (340, 919)
White paintwork	Medium grey (399, 415)
Windows	White (01, White)
Balcony railings, steps, pillars at foot of steps	Black (403, 310)
Brown brickwork squares on gable	Brown (381, 838)

NOTE: The chart has been split (without overlap)
in order to fit it to the page. To make stitching
easier, you may like to enlarge the chart on a
photocopier and join the two halves together.

$\mathscr{S}$TREET $\mathscr{S}$CENES

Now that you have seen how easy it is to design and stitch a picture of just one building, you may wish to try a more challenging project and compose a street scene which reflects your village or town.
For this, you will need to take plenty of photographs. Choose a bright sunny day and stand in positions from which you can see clearly the buildings you like most and, if possible, get 'front on' to them to take your photographs.

The scene we have devised for the design photographed on pages 50-1 shows a market place with a road winding through it; we had to take one or two overall scene shots and several smaller views, then piece them together to get a pleasing composition.

The town we chose has a market place but there was no single angle that would show it against the backdrop of the buildings, so we took shots of separate stalls and placed them at the front of our picture to give the best composition. Using separate shots also meant that we could show individual fruits and vegetables and establish the correct proportion between the size of people and that of the stall.

SETTING THE SCENE

We decided to put in a tree because we are well practised in trees! You will probably notice the similarity between this tree in the street scene and the tree at the left hand side of the Large Formal Garden in Chapter 2. We changed it slightly to give it a more windswept look.

To achieve this we drew sweeping lines on the graph paper and shaded areas to the bottom of each line using coloured pencils in a dark green tone to look like shadow, then shaded the top in light green and left lots of open space to show light coming through. The result is an impression of a tree in the wind. We feel it looks effective.

Next we positioned the houses and shops, then the vegetable stall. The picture needed something in the foreground, so we decided to make a feature of the black metal posts that mark out the pedestrianised area and the bench. The flower tubs were the next good idea, and the people we placed last.

PUTTING IN THE PEOPLE

We used the people that appeared on the photographs, but we could have traced or copied them from a magazine just as easily. The woman and child could not be made to fit around the posts so we moved them. The bigger person had to go in the biggest space we had left on the design. Mother and child were inverted by tracing onto transparent graph paper and then reversing the paper.

We needed someone tending the market stall. Ideally, they had to be bending down to fit into the space, but none of our photographs had such a person so one of our friends had to pose! We sketched her onto graph paper and squared the image off, and it looks just fine. The little 'granny' figure on the bench was drawn entirely from imagination. We felt it just had to be somebody wide, sitting down in a big, floppy coat with a dented-in felt hat. We added the shopping basket to match the image.

We had to make a special trip to find a post box to sketch for the design. The one we found is modern and it would have been nice to have had an older-looking one, but there just wasn't one available.

There is a lot of empty space in the middle of the picture where the road is, but we think it is very effective. It takes the eye along the line of the shops and other buildings to the back of the picture in a relaxed, natural sweep.

STITCHING HINTS

There are a number of technical methods you can use to enhance your design. A varied use of stitching and colour will go a long way to making your design come alive.

PERSPECTIVE AND DETAIL

It is possible to become overwhelmed with trying to show minute details on the buildings. One of the things to remember is that as the buildings recede into the background of the picture, the detail will become less and less obvious and so the outline can become less detailed.

On the white building in the middle of our picture there is quite a lot of detail around the windows, but on the little buildings in the right hand corner in the market place, there is only a hint of outline to show the window positions. None of the details of the glazing is included. This allows the picture to fade out into the distance in a natural-looking way.

Do the same in your picture. The details you want to show are in the foreground. Look at the folds in the clothes of our little old lady who is closest to the viewer. Again, notice the detail on her basket and on the tulips which are in the foreground. This all helps to give a feeling of depth.

ALTERNATE CROSS STITCH

Another use of technique can be seen in our use of alternate cross stitch. In this design we wanted to show the position of the pavements but didn't want them to be as dominant as the buildings. Using alternate cross stitch was the ideal solution.

COLOURS

The colour, you will note, also fades from grey at the front to a lighter creamy colour in the distance. Remember that in paintings, objects in the foreground are usually made darker and brighter, so the people, the post box, the fruit and vegetables are worked in strong colours in our market place design. The buildings in the background are worked in lighter colours to make them less dominant.

AUTHENTIC BUILDINGS

This is your opportunity to experiment with the variety of building styles which usually nudge shoulder to shoulder in all but the newest of towns.

In our example the variety in roof shapes and heights, and the irregular surface created as one building changes into the next, add to the picture's interest and give opportunity for more texture and colour changes for the needlewoman. In some towns the buildings have been renewed over centuries, and to stitch in one tone or one texture or to one scale would not give the authentic look of weathered architecture which has evolved *(continued on page 50)*

CHART 11 Street Scene

slowly. In our line of buildings there is one brick surface in the midst of stucco and stone, and we think this blends appropriately.

We have also varied the dimensions of each building, with a different allocation of visible window, wall and roof space given to each. You will notice that the blue and white building is almost all window space.

We have mentioned previously that paler colours will successfully fade a building into the background and recede the image; one further technique is to reduce the number of strands in the needle so that the texture of the stitched area is lighter. A building cross-stitched in a single strand next to one stitched in two strands will appear to be further away, and perspective is thereby enhanced.

Unless there are severe planning restrictions

INSTRUCTIONS FOR STREET SCENE
The design measures 200 squares by 130 squares. Follow stitch instructions for the Large Formal Garden, page 18.

COLOUR KEY

		Anchor	DMC
/	Stone	393	640
▽	Dark brown	381	838
C	Sandstone	373	437
U	Black	403	310
∩	White	01	White
O	Light grey	399	415
◔	Dark grey	400	317
+	Blue-grey	922	930
I	Off white	830	3033
S	Brick	5975	356
X	Dark green	879	500
▲	Medium green	244	701
●	Light green	241	704
∧	Maroon	22	814
T	Medium blue	137	798
—	Pale yellow	300	745
O	Orange	314	741
V	Purple	102	550

Outlines

People, post box, black and white buildings, tulip containers, red apples, writing on apple sign	Black (403, 310)
Glazing bars on windows, window reflections, name on black and white shop	White (01, white)
Far pavement, yellow awning and stall, surround of apple sign, green apples, grapefruit	Stone (393, 640)
Near pavement, scales	Dark grey (400, 317)
Tulip leaves and stems	Medium green (244, 701)
Tulip flowers	Maroon (22, 814)
Blue and white house	Medium blue (137, 798)
Green awning	Dark green (879, 500)
Basket, name on sandstone and blue shop, off-white awning, oranges, bananas, market boxes and sack	Dark brown (381, 838)

in your chosen area, the colours of paintwork on the wood, stone or brick will be varied. Sometimes this may lead to an ugly clash, and then of course you can use your own taste and judgement to decide upon a more pleasing colour range. Our picture has a simple scheme of white, off white and sandstone, with white or blue paintwork and mostly blue-grey roof tiles.

Stitched Street Scene. Although this design was adapted freely from a series of photographs, it is still recognisable to anyone who knows the market square and its surroundings

· 6 ·

$\mathscr{C}$OME $\mathscr{I}$NSIDE

*If you now feel confident about working outdoor scenes, try
extending your range to depict life inside your house – starting
with the hallway. There are different considerations here. An
individual piece of furniture or an inviting corner requires a
different technique. Following the charts in this chapter will
help you get started.*

THE SEARCH FOR INSPIRATION

Standing in a room, it is never possible to see the whole; your eye naturally flits from object to object and settles on the features it finds most attractive or interesting. Your first task is to choose the features you want to include in your design.

These can be ornaments or furniture or decorative features, but they must be cross stitchable. The outside of a house with its regular verticals and horizontals is relatively easy to draw, chart and stitch. But once you really look at corners of rooms, at curtains and fabrics and chairs, you will realise how many of the outlines are curved.

Your only possibility is to choose carefully and to adapt the shapes as they appear into shapes you can form with cross stitch. Remember you are trying to capture the 'essence' of the furniture or the fireplace, not the geometric reality. Your picture is not going to be a photographic 'copy' but a beautiful interpretation which is atmospheric and evocative. Be prepared to make changes and to use artistic licence.

HOW TO BEGIN

Start by choosing things which are, as far as possible, upright or flat rather than curved or diagonal, and try to stand 'front on' to them to make your sketch or take your photograph. For example, a corner cupboard with a curved front is almost impossible to chart and stitch unless you attempt to show it straight on (Fig 14). But if you do so it will stop looking like a corner cupboard and look like an ordinary flat cupboard!

Better to leave this for now. A more advanced stitcher will, of course, be able to deal with three dimensions, but if this is your first interior then stick to pianos, tables, fireplaces, clocks, lamps, shelves, windows or anything which can be 'straightened' for cross stitch.

The panelling on this dining-room unit (Fig 15), for example, is easy to show in cross stitch. First do a flat stretch of cross stitching, then the outlining on top to form the relief of the panelling. When charting a particular piece of furniture, place yourself directly in front of it so that most of the lines appear horizontal or vertical. The design will then be easier to achieve in cross stitch.

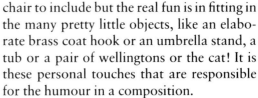

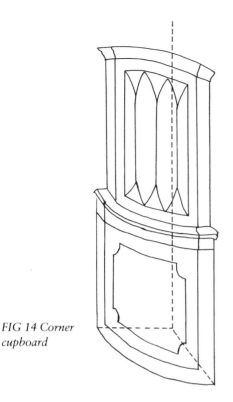

FIG 14 Corner
cupboard

FIG 15 Dining-room unit

ADDING A PERSONAL TOUCH

There aren't many large pieces of furniture that go comfortably in a hall. You may have a clock or a table or a particular favourite chair to include but the real fun is in fitting in the many pretty little objects, like an elaborate brass coat hook or an umbrella stand, a tub or a pair of wellingtons or the cat! It is these personal touches that are responsible for the humour in a composition.

Simple shaped objects are certainly easier to render in cross stitch but if you choose personal objects, even though you may have to simplify their shape, they will add an original and recognisable element to enhance the charm of your design.

Having now reduced everything to straight lines, we are going to suggest you bring back a few natural curves by introducing plant life into your composition.

Plants are brilliant additions, and are generally easy to simplify to just a few crosses. If shown cascading down over furniture, they break the severity of the straight lines and are also an excuse for introducing bright colour.

BOLD MOVES

If you are particularly fond of your curtains and windows and want them in your picture but they are not suitably placed, for example in relation to the fireplace and chair that you want to stitch, then don't hesitate, change their position, for instance by bringing them into the alcove you are depicting so they are included.

We can assure you, this will work: people will recognise the room in your picture from the elements you have brought together, not from their placement.

There are certain distinctive architectural details that can add considerably to your picture and you should try to incorporate them if you can justify doing so. If you have an arch, for example, then by all means include it. Of course, it may be in one room and the fireplace and furniture you want in another, but the principle remains. Put them together, make a collage of different rooms in your house, and the picture will work.

COLOURS AND CONTRASTS

As with the outside of the house, choose colours that are slightly brighter than the colours in the room you want to portray. Follow your basic colour theme, but make the colours and contrast stronger.

If you are stitching the hall and yours is in cream tones with perhaps one or two touches of maroon, then put together threads of these shades but brighter. It might look garish in real life, but in your embroidered picture it won't.

HOW TO CHART THE BASIC LAYOUT

A square hall would be ideal to chart as all your furniture and other objects would have a good chance of fitting into the frame. Most halls, however, are long and thin and the stitcher is not usually able to show the whole thing. This is where ingenuity comes in handy. You may have to choose a different approach, for instance, standing at the bottom of the stairs and looking towards the door. This would be a good choice if you had stained glass in the window panels of your front door.

If, on the other hand, you wanted to feature the staircase you might wish to focus on the newel post or the curving banister. For this you may need to stand at the front door and look towards the stairs.

Stairs can be a challenge, but if you only show part of them, like the edging of the tread, the tiny outline details can make a beautiful effect. Don't try to show the whole thing. Simply 'suggest' the stairs with appropriate lines.

A staircase is dull if you are simply looking from the front, so be prepared to change the angle so that the stairs are just coming in from the side. All that will be seen are the bottom two steps. If there is a banister rail, show that in detail. People will still recognise the picture as being of your hall, even though

the stairs are coming from the wrong side.

Having thought about all the elements you want to include, get started on your chart by drawing out the rectangle measuring approximately 120 by 80 squares. You could work a bigger picture by doubling these dimensions, but the basic shape will give a satisfactory rectangle for you to stitch. Sketch in the basics – usually the stairs and a door; then once you are happy with their positioning, move on to the detail.

If you are using drawings or photographs of the different objects, start thinking of how you can place them onto the rectangle so that they all fit together. As we have stressed, they need not fit as they do in your hall, but so that they look harmonious within the picture.

At the planning stage of a design, after choosing the pieces of furniture and ornaments and placing them against the architectural features, it may still be necessary to revise your ideas. Initially, in our hall design,

Stitched Hall. This picture remains instantly recognisable despite the changes made to the layout during the design process. It captures the feel of the hall, and the trimmings add the personal touch

Barbara had imagined a carved green chair. Playing with the design on the graph paper it became apparent that there was a greater space to fill than would be taken up by a chair. Hence the inclusion of the chaise-longue in the finished picture. Do not be afraid to invent.

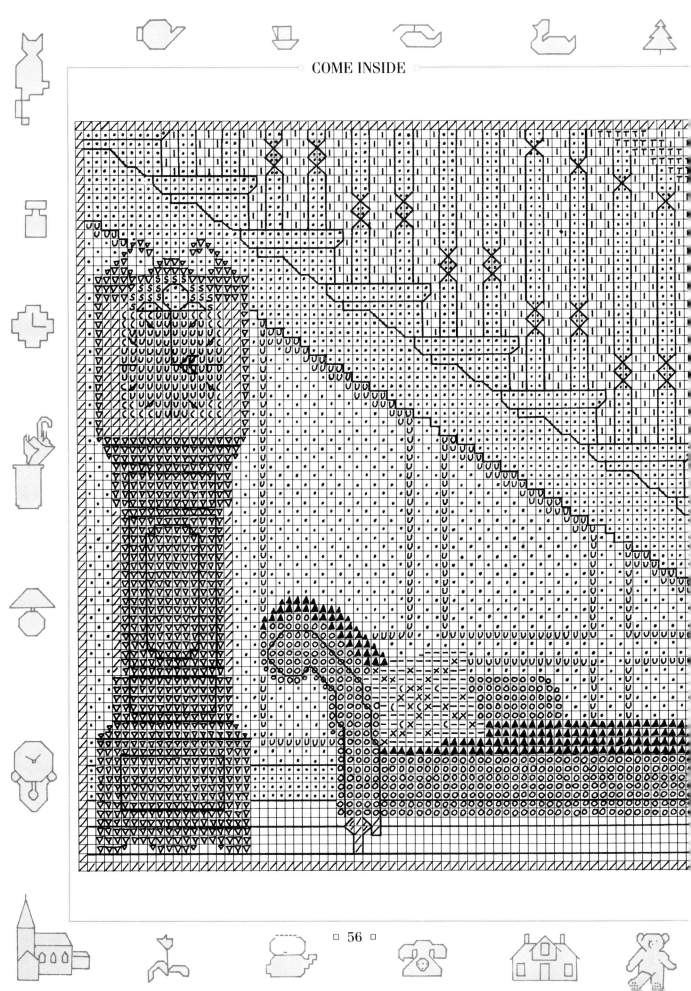

INSTRUCTIONS FOR HALL

The design measures 120 squares by 84 squares. Follow stitch instructions for the Large Formal Garden, page 18.

COLOUR KEY

		Anchor	DMC
/	Dark brown	381	839
▽	Mahogany	351	400
T	Light brown	378	407
●	White	01	White
S	Dark grey	400	317
U	Off white	830	3033
O	Dark green	879	500
▲	Medium green	244	701
I	Light green	241	704
X	Pink	76	603
—	Wine	70	915
C	Gold	307	783

Outlines

Clock, chaise-longue, newel post	Black (403, 310)
Stairs, window, skirting board	Dark grey (400, 317)
Plant pot	Dark green (879, 500)
Floor	Light brown (378, 407)

CHART 12 Hall

OUR HALL DESIGN

For this design (photograph on pp54-5) we wanted to bring in the banister rail and the balustrade because they add fine detail, but not the whole staircase so we decided to show the staircase coming round a corner.

A good starting point for making a change like this is to search magazines and art or decoration books for the image you have in mind. We keep a file of cuttings for reference and found it useful in this case. Looking at our pile of 'staircases' we found one that showed just the bottom of the stairs coming round a corner, so we copied the basic shape onto the graph paper.

We decided not to colour all the woodwork brown, since we wanted the furniture to be brown. To create a contrast, only the banister rail was worked to look like natural wood and the rest was shown as painted white. The whiteness has been effectively broken up with dark grey to show the treads of the stairs and to indicate the fancy carving on the end of each tread.

We found a simple way to make the balusters look cylindrical was to bring in little half stitches to show the turned ornamental detail. This was easily achieved with four half stitches, then two half stitches above and two below (Fig 16).

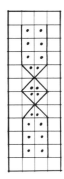

FIG 16 *The rounded contours of the baluster can be implied by the use of diagonal half cross stitch and outlining*

WORKING THE DETAILS

There was still an area of white behind the chaise-longue, so instead of filling in every stitch, we created a more textured look (which was also easier and quicker to sew) by working panels using alternate cross stitch for the in-fill. This stitch, described in Chapter 2, is extremely useful for showing wallpapers, panelling and floors when stitching interiors.

Next, to bring out the panelling, rather than working more outline stitch, we chose an off-white to highlight the position of the panels. In your hall, if the walls are plain white, invent some panelling to add interest, or hang pictures or fill in with wallpaper – anything to break up large, plain areas and give detail will make the finished picture more attractive.

COLOUR CHOICES

We admit that we were very bold in our colour choices for the hall picture, particularly on the stair carpet and the chaise-longue. Our basic colour scheme was green and pink, and if you examine the picture you will see that we have not used many other colours, simply contrasting shades of our two basic colours, with the necessary brown and white of the woodwork and a touch of yellow which comes into the clock, plant pot and window.

To show the treads and uprights of the stairs we chose two very different pinks; a dark wine shade and a light, bright shade. In reality the colour contrast would never be as marked as this, even with the light shining in from above the stairs, but in embroidery anything is possible!

We made the contrast to give the effect of the stairs coming downwards and to break up the solid look of carpet, but the intensity of the colours we used adds considerably to the boldness and glow of the scene.

Similarly on the chaise-longue, we wanted to show it in green, and chose first the light medium green, then combined it with a dark green. You can see that this has worked well, because it makes a good contrast between the seat and the back of the settee.

Hall furniture

HALL FURNITURE AND ACCESSORIES

The use of colour is all-important in portraying stained-glass work. As mentioned earlier, there are key colours suitable for the representation of stained glass – pale blues and greens for background and darker green, wine and gold for motifs. It is impossible to reproduce complex and ornate glass motif designs in a few cross stitches, but with the best use of colour and some outlining, a simple clarity can be achieved.

Draw the pattern, carefully select a few colours and begin to stitch. If it looks disappointing and lacking in clarity at this point, remember that it will come alive with the addition of outlining in the back stitch. Dark grey Anchor 400/DMC 317 will help to add definition, and by using one strand of this colour and working carefully round all the motif outlines, the glass designs will start to take shape. Other details on the door, for example wooden panels and door handles, can also be indicated by using back stitch.

CHAIRS AND TABLES

Dining chairs are three-dimensional objects which are particularly difficult to translate into two-dimensional designs. However, the two examples here show you how it is possible to give some depth to this type of chair if the image is shown from an angle. This does give us the difficulty of dealing with diagonal lines, which means that 'stepping' has to be used (see page 24).

Tables are far easier to deal with than chairs as they can usually be shown from front view and still look like tables. It is not necessary to show depth, or even the back legs in the simplest design, as shown here. To design a tablecloth, look at how the folds appear as lines in a draped cloth, and how the hemline is stepped and uneven. With a liberal use of half stitches, it becomes possible to depict a tablecloth quite well, as shown here.

CLOCK

It can be very difficult to show clock faces. The detail of numbers and hands is impossible to show, and are better hinted at by single lines as shown here. Carving detail on wood can be shown in outline, using black over the light or mid-brown of the wood. The pendulum can be made to look like brass by using a gold shade such as Anchor 307/DMC 783.

Sometimes it becomes impossible to show clear definition if the whole surface of the object is filled in with cross stitch. We overcame this by leaving the inside of the clock case blank, with the pendulum clearly showing. Do not be afraid to leave empty spaces in your designs, as often they add a clarity which cannot be achieved in any other way.

INSTRUCTIONS FOR HALL FURNITURE AND TRIMMINGS

Follow stitch instructions for the Large Formal Garden, page 18.

COLOUR KEY

		Anchor	DMC
▲	Medium pink	895	223
X	Light pink	48	963
I	Wine	70	915
∧	Medium blue	137	798
U	Light blue	975	3753
T	Grey-blue	922	930
/	Dark brown	381	838
C	Medium brown	351	400
S	Light brown	373	437
O	White	01	White
–	Black	403	310
●	Light green	208	563

Outlines

Door, tulip flowers, vase	Dark grey (400, 317)
Clock, small table, telephone, umbrella	Black (403, 310)
Pink-cover table legs, umbrella stand	Dark brown (381, 838)
Plant	Dark green (879, 500)
Plant pot	Grey-blue (922, 930)
Tulip leaves	Light green (208, 563)
Table cloth	Medium pink (895, 223)

CHART 13
Hall Furniture and
Trimmings

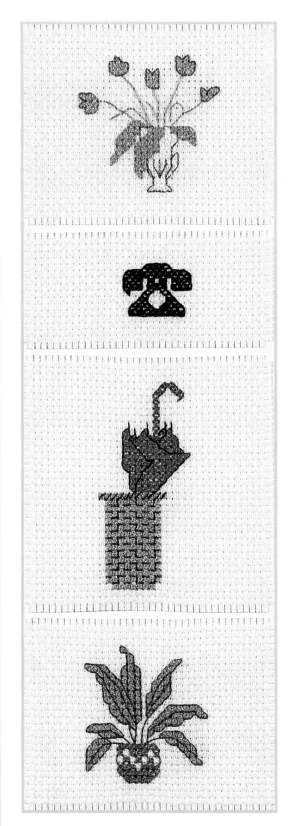

POT PLANT AND VASE OF FLOWERS

When choosing accessories to fill a picture of a hall, there are two main points to consider.

Firstly, to make these accessories fit in as parts of the whole picture, stitch them in colours already used in the main objects. Secondly, it is not necessary to copy exactly from an actual object. For pot plants and flower vases, for example, try experimenting with shapes on graph paper, choosing one that pleases you and fills the space.

Try to have as little overlapping of leaves and flowers as possible, or they will become a blur. In choosing a green for the leaves, either select a medium to dark shade to stand on its own, or a lighter shade to be outlined in a darker shade, with a hint of 'veins' indicated in single strands of thread. Never attempt to show all the veins on a leaf or all the leaves on a plant, as this will only result in over-crowding.

TELEPHONE

Although it is a relatively small item, the telephone has a compact shape of single colour which translates quite well into cross stitch. It may be made larger or smaller, to fit into the available space. The dial need not be shown in any detail, but can be represented sufficiently by a contrasting colour.

UMBRELLA STAND

Walking sticks and umbrellas are not particularly easy to depict unless they are standing bolt upright, which is not what they naturally do when placed in a holder, although umbrellas do have some width to take the eye away from the slightly unnatural vertical of the handle.

We have stitched the holder to look like basketwork, in order to give it some interest and texture. The basketweave effect is achieved with short back stitches representing the woven strands.

· 7 ·

THE KITCHEN

In a kitchen design, the furniture is actually more important than the architecture of the room. A design representing either a traditional Victorian kitchen or a modern completely fitted kitchen will achieve the desired effect by showing the furniture in detail rather than the background. The stitcher has to consider ways of making the furniture and fittings as interesting as possible. The techniques discussed in the previous chapters will be essential.

KITCHEN PERSPECTIVES

In the Yellow Dresser Kitchen design (see pages 64-7), we have shown the end wall at the back of the picture and one side wall coming down one side of the design. Working out the perspective was a challenge.

An easier way would have been to place objects, for instance, a table, an Aga, a cupboard and a dresser either in a row or stepped up or down from each other, and just show the contours of the furniture rather than those of the room. However, our example shows you how to try to incorporate the contours of the room with the units built around.

The starting point was to take some photographs of a friend's large and beautiful kitchen. There were lots of pretty, interesting objects dotted around the room, begging to be stitched. Some of the photographs were, as we have advised you before, taken 'straight on' to an individual piece and in close-up, so that the detail and the line were clear. Other shots were taken from further

back to show how the units down the side-walls fitted into the kitchen.

Although there are tiles in the original kitchen, we decided to stitch floorboards in the picture. This was principally to help the perspective; it also gives depth to the room. Vertical lines were sewn in the centre and as we stitched away from the centre, we tilted the lines out at increasing angles. This was achieved simply by trial and error, by holding a strand of cotton in the position we felt right, then stitching, but we feel it has worked. These lines are not perfectly evenly spaced but they do give the feeling of depth and lead the eye into the back of the picture.

CHARTING THE DESIGN

To make a satisfactory design based on our friend's kitchen, we had to use our imagination and reposition some of the units. The glass-fronted top cupboard that appears on the right in the design was originally on the left in the photographs, but we repositioned it in the only place it could be fitted.

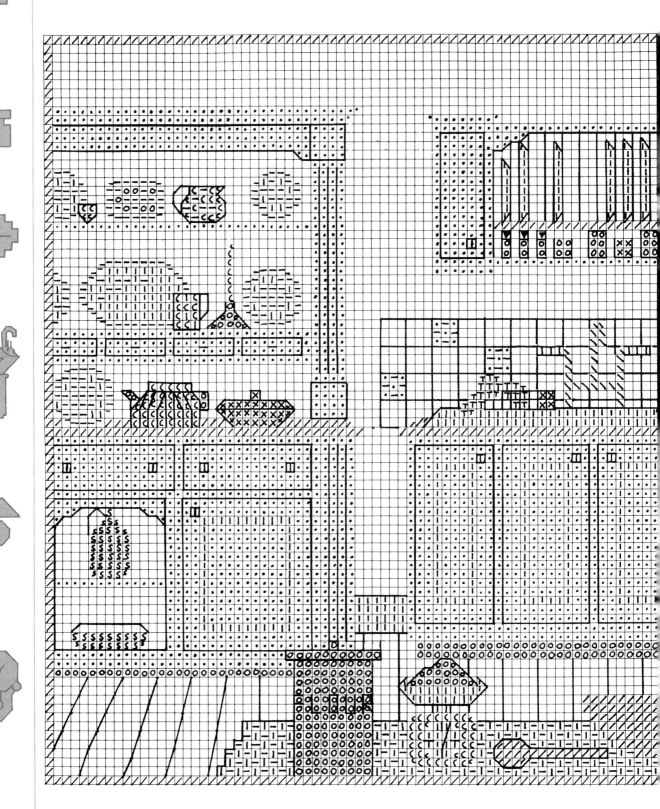

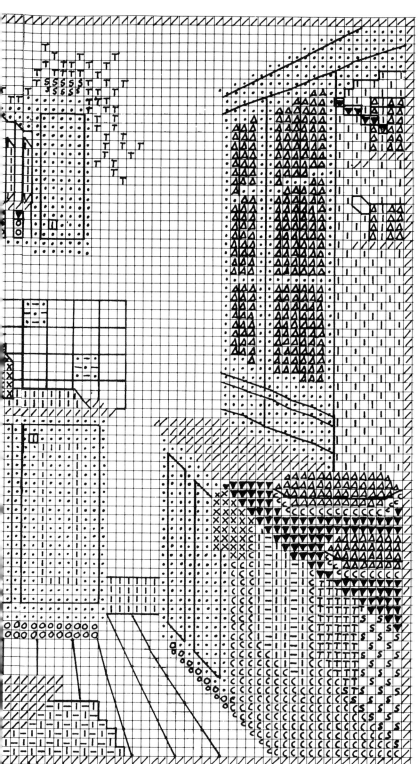
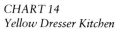

INSTRUCTIONS FOR YELLOW DRESSER KITCHEN

The design measures 120 squares by 84 squares. Follow stitch instructions for the Large Formal Garden, page 18.

COLOUR KEY

		Anchor	DMC
●	Yellow	300	745
O	Off white	830	3033
C	Dark blue	149	336
—	Medium blue	137	798
X	Pale blue	975	3753
/	Brown	373	437
△	Light grey	399	415
▼	Dark grey	400	317
T	Green	208	563
I	White	01	White
S	Terracotta	5975	356
\	Gold – Anchor Effektgarn (use three strands)		

Outlines

Glazing bars on cupboard, tea cosy	Yellow (300, 745)
Sink tidy, table cloth, white plates, yellow units	Medium blue (137, 798)
Terracotta pottery	Terracotta (5975, 356)
Dark blue pottery	Dark blue (149, 336)
Plate rack	Brown (373, 437)
All other outlines	Dark grey (400, 317)

CHART 14
Yellow Dresser Kitchen

We wanted to show front views of the sink unit with its lovely taps, the plate rack and the dresser, but since this would leave no space in this size of picture to show both sides of the room, we restricted ourselves to showing just one side, the right-hand side, with all the bits of furniture we wanted to include.

The Aga is in the foreground, then the glass-fronted cupboard. There was a remaining problem: this arrangement created empty floor space in the foreground. This was filled by showing a top slice of the table. The plain brown wood colour of the real table would have been too dull, so we showed it covered by a blue cloth, which also balances the predominant yellow colour of the units and fits in with the colour scheme of this kitchen.

ORNAMENTS AND DETAILS

There are a lot of details in this kitchen which give interest and make this a particularly busy picture. All the pottery and ornaments on the dresser come out well when stitched. We put the tea cosy onto the dresser because it seemed a good contrast, but we had to change the colour from the original.

In real life this is a lived-in kitchen with lots of mess, but when stitched the clutter was eliminated. As a result the design then looked rather clinical. One solution was to introduce a plant. We positioned one on top of the unit and this had a softening effect.

Needless to say, our friend was delighted with this 'ideal' version of her busy kitchen.

The Yellow Dresser and Pine Dresser Kitchen designs look perfectly at home displayed here amongst the flowers and crockery in a country kitchen. These pictures demonstrate the different effects achieved through a complex use of perspective (right-hand side of the Yellow Dresser design) and a simpler, 'straight-on' approach

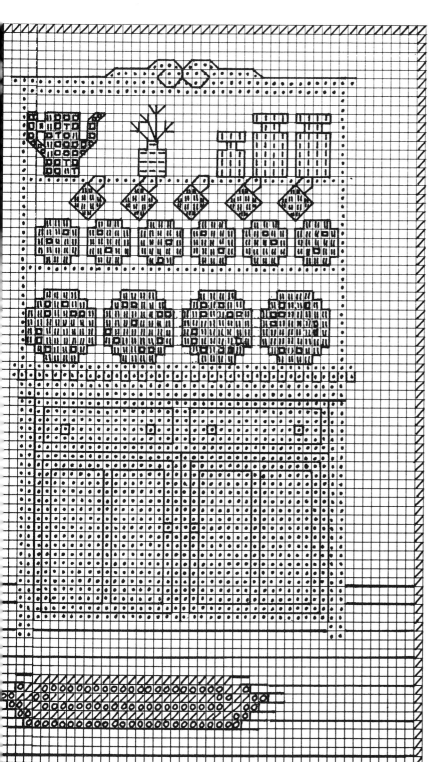

INSTRUCTIONS FOR PINE DRESSER

The design measures 120 squares by 84 squares. Follow stitch instructions for the Large Formal Garden, page 18.

COLOUR KEY

		Anchor	DMC
/	Dark green	879	500
X	Medium green	244	701
O	Light green	241	704
S	Dark brown	381	838
△	Medium brown	351	400
●	Light brown	373	437
U	Terracotta	340	919
T	Pink	895	223
‖	Medium blue	130	799
I	Pale blue	975	3753
—	Dark grey	400	317
□	White	01	White
\	Gold – Anchor Effektgarn (use three strands)		

Outlines

Dresser, lamp	Dark brown (381, 838)
Picture string	Medium brown (351, 400)
Window, floor, wall	Light brown (373, 437)
Picture, plant, tablecloth	Medium green (244, 701)
Clock	Black (403, 310)
Objects on dresser	Dark grey (400, 317)
Mat, stems of flowers on dresser	Dark green (879, 500)
Petals of flowers on dresser	Pink (895, 223)

CHART 15
Pine Dresser Kitchen

MORE KITCHEN PICTURES

In two of our other examples of stitched kitchen pictures the Aga design is the same but the surround gives each a different look. These are all simpler designs than the Yellow Dresser Kitchen, since we just placed the furniture into a room shape with no particular regard for perspective.

In the 'Pine Dresser' and the 'Red Aga' we included a corner of the room to give a little depth, but in the 'Green Aga' the image is just charted against one flat wall and this is perfectly acceptable in cross stitch. The end result looks rather naive, but there is a charm to flat, primitive cross stitch. Early samplers show furniture looking very similar to this. The table and chairs in the Green Aga picture are reminiscent of Victorian or earlier European cross stitch sampler style, and have great appeal.

The Red and Green Aga designs show just how effective a simple 'straight-on' view can be when worked in cross stitch. The pictures have a naive charm which compliments the solid shape of the Aga cookers perfectly

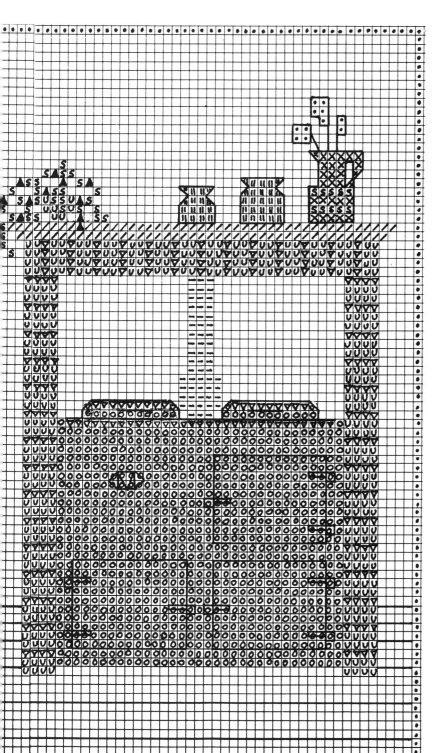

INSTRUCTIONS FOR RED AGA

The design measures 120 squares by 84 squares. Follow stitch instructions for the Large Formal Garden, page 18.

COLOUR KEY

		Anchor	DMC
●	Dark brown	351	400
/	Pinkish brown	378	407
U	Brick red	5975	356
—	Black	403	310
O	Maroon	22	814
X	Pink	895	223
S	Light green	241	704
▲	Dark green	879	500
‖	Pale blue	975	3753
□	Orange	314	741
▽	Grey	400	317
V	Copper	340	919

Outlines

Aga, cupboards, tea caddy	Black (403, 310)
Pots on shelves, dresser	Dark grey (400, 317)
Floor, window	Yellowish brown (373, 437)
Wooden spoons	Dark brown (351, 400)
Kettle	Copper (340, 919)
Stool	Maroon (22, 814)
Stems of flowers on dresser	Dark green (879, 500)
Petals of flowers on dresser	Pink (895, 223)
Blind (work alternate rows as illustrated)	Maroon and light green

CHART 16
Red Aga Kitchen

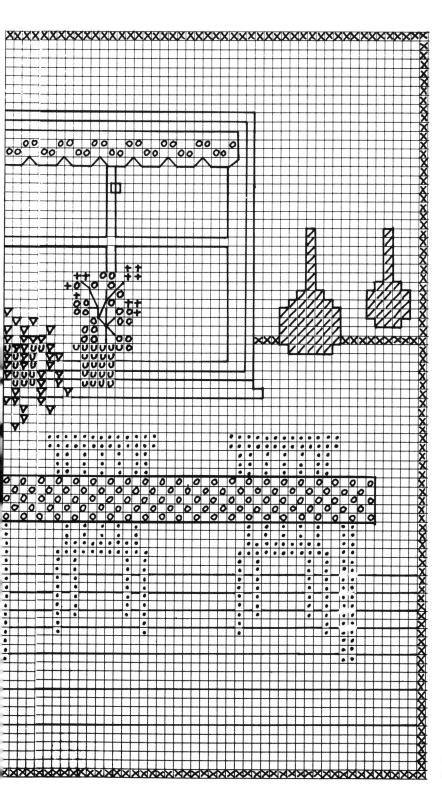

INSTRUCTIONS FOR GREEN AGA

The design measures 126 squares by 84 squares. Follow stitch instructions for the Large Formal Garden, page 18.

COLOUR KEY

		Anchor	DMC
▲	Dark green	879	500
O	Medium green	244	701
▽	Pale green	241	704
X	Medium brown	378	407
●	Light brown	373	437
U	Terracotta	340	919
/	Copper	5975	356
S	Yellow	307	783
■	White	01	White
T	Pale blue	975	3753
+	Red	333	606
‖	Light grey	399	415
—	Black	403	310

Outlines

Cupboard	Dark brown (381, 838)
Floorboards	Medium brown (378, 407)
Blind, tablecloth, plant	Medium green (244, 701)
Saucepans, bottles on shelf	Dark grey (400, 317)
Window	Light grey (399, 415)
Scales, Aga	Black (403, 310)
Cat	White (01, White)

CHART 17
Green Aga Kitchen

· 8 ·

*C*OSY *C*ORNERS

It is possible to create a pleasing design by focusing upon a single feature rather than a whole room. A fireplace motif is obvious and compelling, with universal appeal, but there are many other possibilities. We hope that the examples in this chapter will show that you don't have to include much to create an atmosphere of comfort.

Should you want inspiration for a particular atmosphere or seasonal arrangement then, as we have suggested before, quality magazines that specialise in homes and gardens are a useful resource. The technique is simply to choose and trace, then transfer the design onto squared paper as we have shown in Chapter 2.

CAT BY FIRE DESIGN

This design consists of simply a fireplace, an easy chair, and a cat. Black cats always stand out well in stitched pictures and give an instant homely feel.

Having placed the fireplace, the cosy chair and the cat in the fireglow, we noticed there was an empty area in the top left corner. The choice of the wreath decoration allows the warm glow of the hearth to be reflected back from the walls.

There are not too many colours in this setting. We limited ourselves to blues and peaches so as to enhance the relaxed feel. The fireplace is in two shades of grey and the simple black outlining gives an illusion of it being incredibly intricate. It is not.

In this composition the key elements of the

fire, the cat, and the armchair, are brought close together. The cat is obviously enjoying the fireglow, and the chair has a plumped cushion angled invitingly towards the on-looker. We have the feeling of looking in on a private moment, perhaps at the end of the day; the fire is lit and the chair awaits.

The picture creates a sense of time suspended, just as these key elements are suspended in space. With such a design you may find it useful to let the elements just 'touch' each other, as we have done. This overlap gives a sense of wholeness and unifies the image.

GREY FIREPLACE DRAWING ROOM

After you have worked on a cosy corner or 'vignette', you may like to try to complete a scene which gives the impression of a whole room. Our 'Grey Fireplace' drawing room scene (see page 79) is a perfect example of a view which gives the key elements of a room: the walls, window, fireplace and furniture in harmony.

Each element has interest. The wallpaper design enlivens the flat surface of the wall; the fireplace is wonderfully decorated with

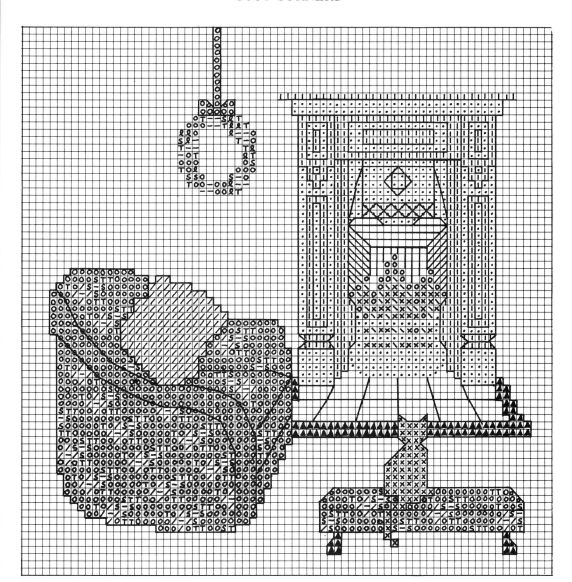

CHART 18 Cat by fire

INSTRUCTIONS FOR CAT BY FIRE

The design measures approximately 70 squares by 70 squares. Follow stitch instructions for the Large Formal Garden, page 18.

COLOUR KEY

		Anchor	DMC
●	Dark grey	400	317
I	Light grey	399	415
S	Blue-grey	922	930
—	Dark peach	9575	353
O	Light peach	4146	3774

		Anchor	DMC
/	Blue	130	799
X	Black	403	310
T	Green	208	563
\	Maroon	22	814
ℓ	Rust	5975	353
▲	Brown	351	400

Outlines

Fireplace, cat	Black (403, 310)
Bow, chair, stool upholstery, hearth tiles	Dark grey (400, 317)
Stool legs, fender	Brown (351, 400)

patterned tiles, and by the outlining which represents the carvings on the original Edwardian cast-iron fireplace surround. The armchair has a traditional woven look to its upholstery, as do the curtains and carpets which are differently textured (note the use of alternate cross stitch again), but which are all unified by colour. Peach, blue, green and grey tones dominate in all the furnishings and features, and give the picture its gentle and welcoming feel. Although the room is 'traditional', the colours are the softer shades currently preferred in interior decoration.

Cat by Fire. A small picture can be every bit as effective as a larger one. Just a few, well-chosen elements create the atmosphere of homely warmth in this design

(Opposite): *The Grey Fireplace Drawing Room contains many examples of patterning depicted in cross stitch: on the tiles, the wallpaper, curtains and upholstery fabric. A careful choice of colours unifies the design, and creates a gentle, welcoming feel*

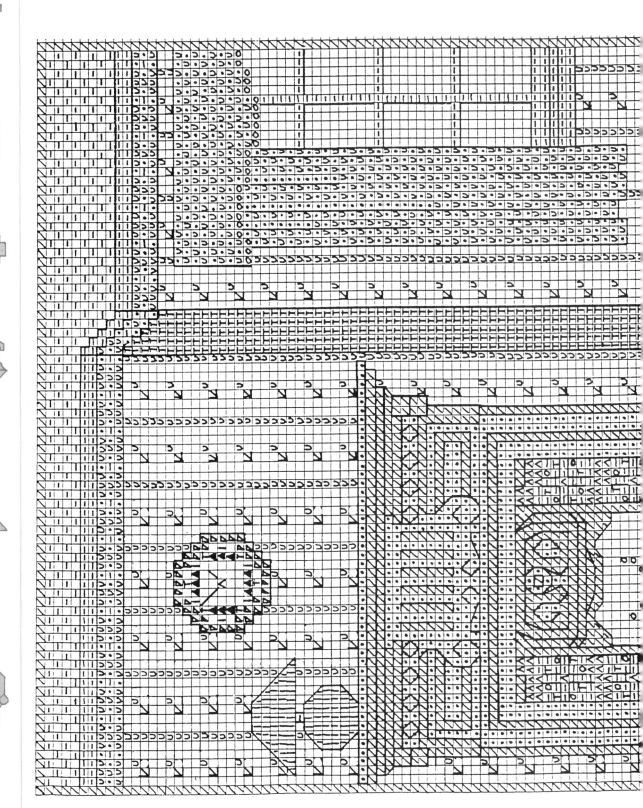

CHART 19 Grey Fireplace Drawing Room

Outlines

Ceiling, walls, skirting board, window, curtain, lamp	Dark grey (400, 317)
Fireplace tiles, coalscuttle, hearth tiles, clock	Dark brown (381, 838)
Fireplace, chair, cushion	Black (208, 563)
Leaves on wallpaper	Light green (208, 563)

	Anchor	DMC
	378	407
	01	White
	922	930
	130	799
	403	310
	208	563

INSTRUCTIONS FOR GREY FIREPLACE DRAWING ROOM

The design measures 84 squares by 120 squares. Follow stitch instructions for the Large Formal Garden, page 18.

COLOUR KEY

		Anchor	DMC
/	Dark grey	400	317
	Light grey	399	415
●	Dark peach	9575	353
T	Light peach	4146	3774
Λ	Dark brown	381	838

▽	Light brown
—	White
O	Blue grey
I	Light blue
S	Black
▲	Light green

CUP OF TEA DESIGN

In our third example, the colour theme is pink and maroon. The furniture is a simple table and chair with a cup and saucer. In the background is the window. Having positioned these features, we felt the grouping still needed something to bring the whole together. We chose to stitch in horizontal lines to give the impression of floorboards. The finished result is rather 1930s looking, but again soft in colour and style.

Table and Chair. The choice of colour plays a very important role in creating atmosphere in a small design. Keeping the colour scheme simple but warm, as in this example, enhances the subject matter

CHART 20 Table and Chair

INSTRUCTIONS FOR CUP OF TEA

The design measures approximately 70 squares by 70 squares. Follow stitch instructions for the Large Formal Garden, page 18.

Outlines

Chair, cushions	Black (403, 310)
Window	Dark grey (400, 317)
Crockery	Medium blue (137, 798)
Tablecloth	Medium pink (895, 223)
Floor	Stone (393, 640)

COLOUR KEY

		Anchor	DMC
●	Wine	70	915
O	Pale pink	48	963
T	Medium pink	895	223
S	Dark pink	76	603
/	Brown	378	407
X	Pale blue	975	3753
—	Blue	130	799
I	Turquoise	185	964
C	White	01	White

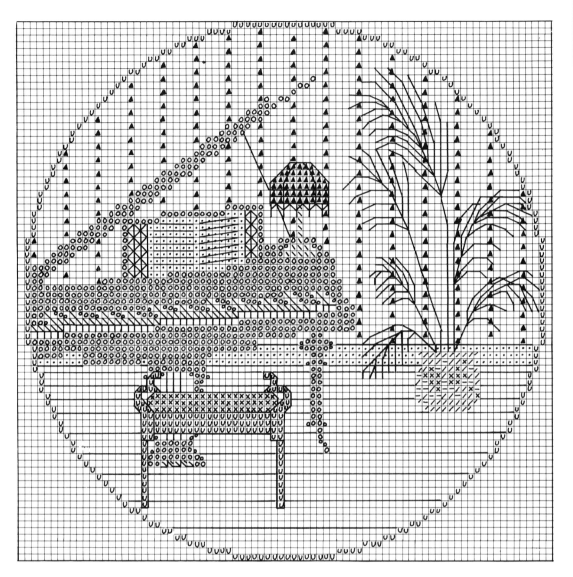

CHART 21   Piano

INSTRUCTIONS FOR PIANO

The design measures 80 squares by 80 squares. Follow stitch instructions for the Large Formal Garden, page 18.

		Anchor	DMC
/	Dark green	879	500
−	Light green	241	704

COLOUR KEY

		Anchor	DMC
●	White	01	White
O	Black	403	310
U	Dark brown	381	838
I	Light brown	373	437
X	Dark pink	895	223
▲	Pale pink	48	963

Outlines

Plant	Medium green (244, 701)
Skirting board	Dark grey (400, 317)
Floor	Light brown (373, 437)
Lamp	Dark pink (895, 223)
Music, piano, stool	Black (403, 310)

Chart 22   Plant in Window

INSTRUCTIONS FOR PLANT IN WINDOW

The design measures 80 squares by 80 squares. Follow stitch instructions for the Large Formal Garden, page 18.

		Anchor	DMC
▲	Mid blue	137	798
U	Brown	381	838
\	Dark green	879	500

COLOUR KEY

		Anchor	DMC
O	Off white	830	3033
—	White	01	White
●	Green	208	563
I	Yellow	300	745
X	Pale blue	975	3753
T	Light blue	130	799

Outlines

Plant	Dark green (879, 500)
Plant stand	Brown (381, 838)
All other outlines	Dark grey (400, 317)

PIANO DESIGN

Another way of showing part of a room is to take a peep-hole view. You can form a circle with your thumb and forefinger to peep through and survey a real room until you find a collection of objects you want to stitch in a pleasing relationship.

Again you can apply this technique to any magazine images and it may help to define something which you think would work. We used this method for our 'Piano' design and the 'Plant in Window' design.

In the piano setting the colours, the frondy

Piano. If you are charting a large item, such as a piano, it is easier to make a tracing from a photograph, provided the angle is suitable, than to try to sketch from life

palm, the lamp, the grand piano and the dots on the wallpaper like little dangling beads all combine to give the picture an Art Nouveau look. A grand piano is quite a difficult thing to sew. This is one shown at a slight angle and the keyboard has had to be stepped; however, no one could doubt that it is clearly a piano.

PLANT IN
WINDOW DESIGN

Windows and curtains shown in combination with the furniture are always successful, as they provide opportunity to include softening, sweeping curves. The plant near the window gives a fresh, natural feel to the overall design.

It is difficult to show items as if through a window in cross stitch but an indoor plant will always soften a picture. Floral patterns on the chairs can be suggested by dotting a few cross stitches around in shades that

Plant in Window. The circular outline to this design surrounds the scene and makes it look even more cosy

'tone'. Alternate cross stitch is used on the floor, which gives a contrasting texture between the floor and the walls.

The circular outline works well here, but it would not be suitable for all pictures. To chart the outline, draw the circle onto graph paper using a pair of compasses. Then, following the circle as closely as possible, shade in individual squares close to the line, so that you finish up with just one row of squares all the way round.

· 9 ·

$\mathcal{T}$HE $\mathcal{B}$ATHROOM

*Bathrooms can provide endless inspiration for cross stitch
pictures. There are so many clear and pleasing shapes to be
charted from the fixtures and fittings, and a wealth of detail in
the accessories you are bound to come across. Try working
your own bathroom design – it's good, clean fun!*

GREEN BATHROOM DESIGN

We chose to design a reproduction Victorian
bathroom with a free-standing, roll-top bath
which was not boxed in (see page 90). This
could have been stitched in pastel shades but
we chose bold colours similar to those the
Victorians used, so as to add a period feel.
Along with the other large items, it produces
a solid, clean-cut effect, with bold shapes and
uncluttered lines, perfect for decoration.
And what really makes this design interesting are all the bits and pieces: the gold taps,
the tooth mug, the bottles and potions that
furnish everyone's bathroom, as well as the
traditional spider plant that thrives in so
many bathrooms too. These details are useful counterpoints to the straight lines of the
sturdy, old-fashioned porcelain.

Once we had placed the large items and
details, we introduced a feeling of depth by
recessing the wall behind the hand basin.
This was achieved by setting the wall back or
rather, slightly higher on the chart, and stepping up the skirting board, then filling in the
small side wall this created with solid, darker
colour. This colour was chosen to tone in
with that of the bath, and add harmony to
the composition.

YOUR OWN DESIGN

The photographs and charts shown here
should give you plenty of ideas for charting
and working your own bathroom design.

INSTRUCTIONS FOR BATHROOM FITTINGS
Follow stitch instructions for the Large Formal
Garden, page 18.

COLOUR KEY

		Anchor	DMC
●	White	01	White
–	Light brown	373	437
I	Pale blue	975	3753
C	Light blue	130	799
T	Dark blue	137	149
/	Off white	830	3033
U	Pale pink	48	963
X	Green	185	964
▲	Mahogany	351	400
V	Light grey	399	415
O ·	Gold – Anchor Effektgarn (use three strands)		

Outlines

Taps, washbasins, bath outlines, loo outlines	Dark grey (400, 317)
Loo decoration	Dark blue (137, 149)
Loo chain	Gold (Effektgarn)
Bath leaf design	Green (185, 964)
Bath flower design	Pink (48, 963)

CHART 23
Bathroom Fittings

Green Bathroom. Leaving unstitched areas, as on the panelling and on the floor, kept this design looking bright and fresh – just right for a bathroom

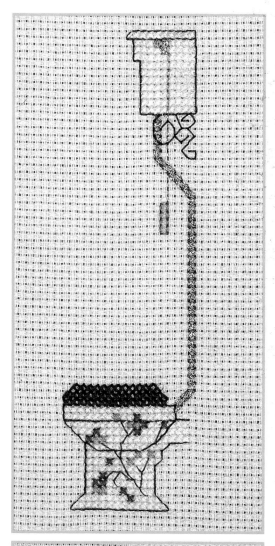

There are not many large items to choose from when designing a bathroom picture, so try to incorporate some interesting detail in the stitching. An ordinary, high-level cistern loo can be turned into a grand feature by adding some flowery patterns

An antique washstand is very satisfying to stitch, and looks just right in a period bathroom picture, with its straight lines and solid areas of porcelain. The turned legs and the back of the wooden surround are highlighted with outline stitch

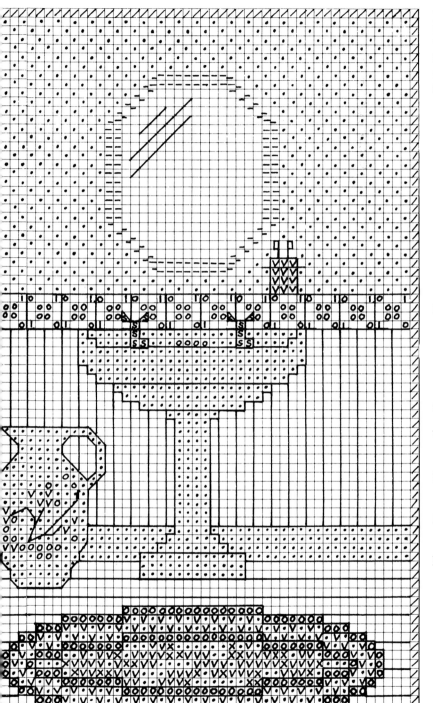

INSTRUCTIONS FOR GREEN BATHROOM

The design measures 120 squares by 84 squares. Follow stitch instructions for the Large Formal garden, page 18.

COLOUR KEY

		Anchor	DMC
●	White	01	White
/	Dark grey	400	317
V	Wine	70	915
O	Light green	241	704
I	Turquoise	185	964
—	Dark green	879	500
X	Pale blue	975	3753
S	Gold – Anchor Effektgarn (use three strands)		

Outlines

Bottles on shelf, taps, wash basin, skirting board, wall corners, bath, tooth mug, rug, picture, curtains, toothbrush bristles	Dark grey (400, 317)
One toothbrush, large jug, tiles	Wine (70, 915)
Window, floor, plant, other toothbrush	Dark green (879, 500)
Lower walls	Light green (241, 704)
Mirror	Pale blue (975, 3753)
Floor	Brown (373, 437)

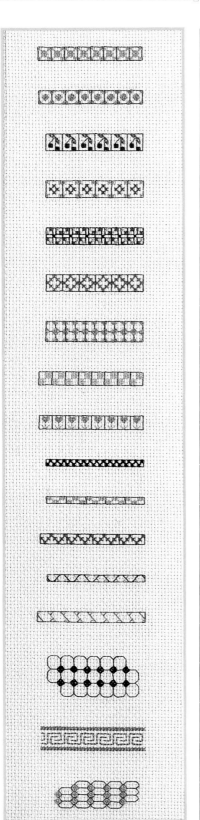

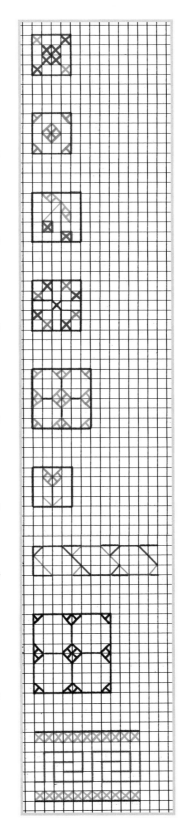

SAMPLER OF CERAMIC TILES

1 *A simple, but effective combination of cross stitch and unstitched areas. You don't need to fill in every square on such a small design*

2 *It looks as though there is a circle in the middle of the tile, but the chart shows how this is produced with diagonal half cross stitch (see Fig 4, page 11)*

3 *Half stitches form the leaf shape and red-out-lined squares the cherries*

4 *The design for this traditional, Dutch-style tile was copied from a fireplace tile. It looks complicated, but is very easy to stitch*

5 *Like 2, this tile is worked entirely with half cross stitch, but the tile is bigger and the colours alternated. The use of outlining makes it look like four small tiles joined together*

6 *The tulip flowers are worked in vertical half cross stitch (see Fig 5A, page 11), and the leaves are in back stitch*

7 *A row of edging tiles like this one would look just right around a bath or mirror, or as a dado trim in a bathroom. Here the outline is stitched in two colours*

8 *This is the same design as in (7), but when worked all in black it looks like a Roman tile, or perhaps a floor tile*

9 *This lovely design is easily stitched using two rows of cross stitch, and is one of the few examples in this book for which we have used two strands for outlining*

STITCHING IN TILES AND DECOR

Tiles are perfect things to cross stitch since they are square and usually patterned with geometric designs in clear, bright colours. There are plenty of ideas for tile designs in the photograph opposite, with a selection charted alongside to get you started.

Choose carefully where to place the tiles in your design. If you were to stitch as many as you might have in your bathroom you would lose the clarity of the picture as a whole, so be selective. We placed one row of tiles along the room at about the level of a dado rail. This arrangement allowed us to show changes of texture. If the white wall had been left either blank or filled in completely it would not have been interesting. The use of alternate cross stitch in white lends texture, while beneath the tiles, the wood panelling is merely suggested by rows of back stitch just two squares apart in the chosen colour, green. By not stitching this area densely, we avoided the picture becoming 'bottom heavy'.

The skirting board is solid and white, but the floorboards are again represented in back stitch. A mat is always useful on a floor like this as it allows all the colours of the composition to be brought together within one small focus. Green, blue, white and maroon are all featured here. It also uses up the odd bits of left-over thread!

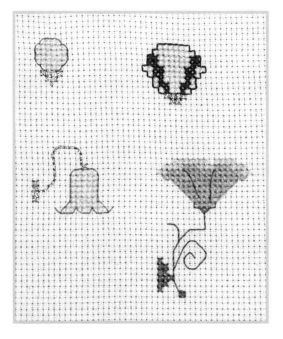

Lighting. Metallic thread in silver or gold is suitable for stitching light fittings, but use it sparingly. Stick to pale colours for the lamp shades, and show detail with darker outline stitch

Mirrors. If you include a mirror in your design, only the frame will really show so make a feature of it. The most effective way of working the mirror itself is to outline stitch the bevelled edge with a single strand of very pale blue. You can hint at the reflective surface with a few lines of back stitch in the same colour. This technique is also useful for showing window glass.

THE BATHROOM

INSTRUCTIONS FOR LIGHTING

Follow stitch instructions for the Large Formal Garden, page 18.

COLOUR KEY

		Anchor	DMC
O	Light blue	130	799
●	Pale pink	48	963
/	Pale blue	975	3753
—	Yellow	300	745
I	Bronze	393	640
U	Maroon	22	814
X	Gold – Anchor Effektgarn (use three strands)		

Outlines

Yellow light, blue light base	Bronze (393, 640)
Maroon and pink light	Maroon (22, 814)
Pink light	Mid pink (895, 223)
Blue light shade	Dark grey (400, 317)

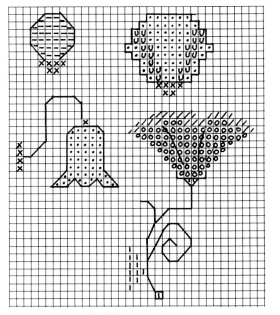

CHART 26   Mirrors

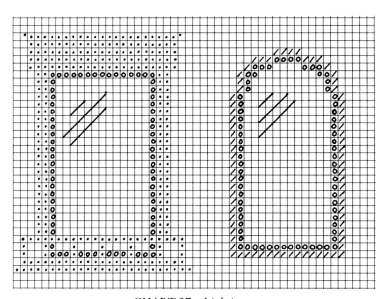

CHART 27   Lighting

INSTRUCTIONS FOR MIRRORS

Follow stitch instructions for the Large Formal Garden, page 18.

COLOUR KEY

		Anchor	DMC
●	Brown	351	400
O	Pale blue	975	3753
/	Gold – Anchor Effektgarn (use three strands)		

Outlines

All outlines	Pale blue (975, 3753)

10

THE BEDROOM

You might imagine that there was little difference between working a bathroom picture and a bedroom picture, but the problems are really quite distinct. Instead of the clean straight lines of ceramic fittings, you will be dealing mainly with soft furnishings and textiles. In this chapter we show you how to chart and work them convincingly, and how to design a pleasing bedroom scene.

Bedroom pictures are not easy because the dominant item of furniture in the room is the bed, and beds present design problems. If placed in the middle of the picture, a bed does tend to take up most of the space, so the perspective must be right – the head must appear smaller than the foot, which is nearest to the onlooker.

The best way to deal with this is to use magazine pictures for reference and find a picture of a bed which is about the size of the one you want on your design – and that is shown straight-on to the camera. Trace the outline, then transfer to graph paper as explained in Chapter 2. This way you can be sure the perspective will be correct.

An alternative would be to move the bed down into the corner of the picture and only show part of it. This way you will be left with plenty of space for all the other personal items in the body of the room. In our example on page 98 we have shown a single bed in position on a chart. This can be used as a starting point for your own bedroom design: the photograph on page 106 shows the same bed adapted to suit an entirely different style.

The photographs and charts on pages 98– 106 show a wide range of bedroom furnishings and fittings – right down to traditional items for a nursery. These can be copied exactly, or used as starting points for your own designs.

Our collection of curtains and blinds on pages 98-9 shows the possibilities for introducing a solid area of colour with texture into any room setting. All these samples avoid the unrealistic regularity which could result if they were stitched without an eye for the detail of how a fabric 'hangs' when drawn back, bunched over a tie-back or dropped flat against the window as a blind. Trial and error stitching may be needed to get the right impression of weight and volume for the look you wish to create – although you will find that generally stronger shades require strong outline colours, while pastels can be outlined in softer tones – but it is this individualistic approach which will produce the most effective results.

There is no rule book to follow when designing in cross stitch – all the effects we illustrate here were the result of trial and error, stitching and looking. You will enjoy the discoveries you make as you work.

Single bed. Moving this bed down to the corner of the chart makes it less dominant in the design. You can use up odds and ends of different coloured thread on the patchwork quilt, or work it in spots, stripes or any other brightly coloured design that takes your fancy

Festoon Blind. Use of outline makes this design very realistic. Breaking up the stripe is simply a matter of shifting the band of colour one square to the left or right, to create the effect of folds at the bottom of the blind

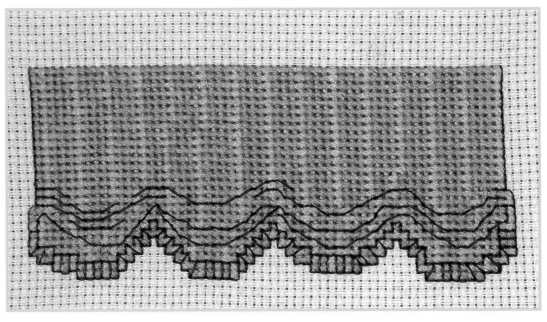

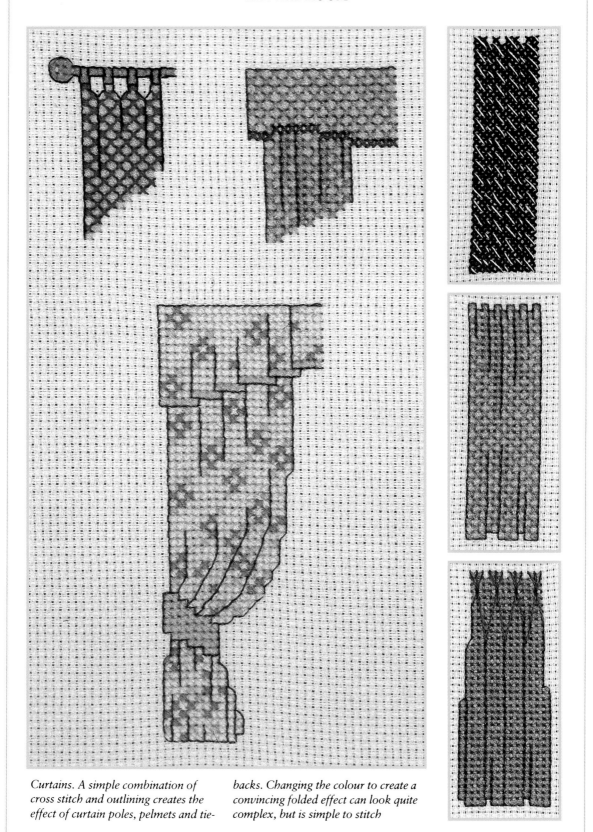

Curtains. A simple combination of cross stitch and outlining creates the effect of curtain poles, pelmets and tie-backs. Changing the colour to create a convincing folded effect can look quite complex, but is simple to stitch

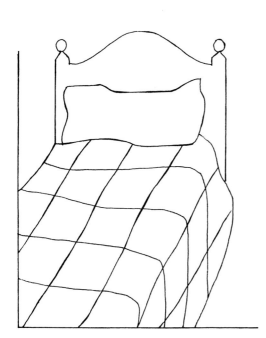

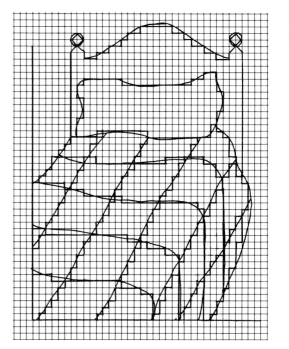

INSTRUCTIONS FOR BLINDS AND CURTAINS

Follow stitch instructions for the large Formal Garden, page 18.

CHART 28 Single bed
This chart shows exactly how 'squaring off' has been used to chart the bed and patchwork quilt shown in the sketch

COLOUR KEY

		Anchor	DMC
V	Light brown	373	437
▲	Dark pink	895	223
·	Light pink	48	963
/	Peach	4146	3774
0	Light grey	399	415
T	Dark grey	400	317
—	Turquoise	185	964
U	Terracotta	340	919

Outlines

Curtain rail and curtains — Dark brown (381, 838)

Festoon blind and outlines, all folds and all other outlines — Dark grey (400, 317)

CHART 29 Festoon blind

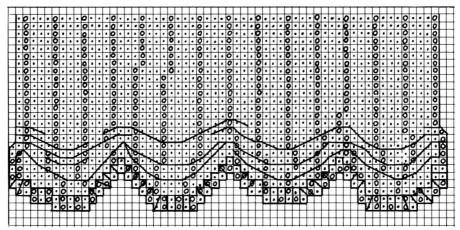

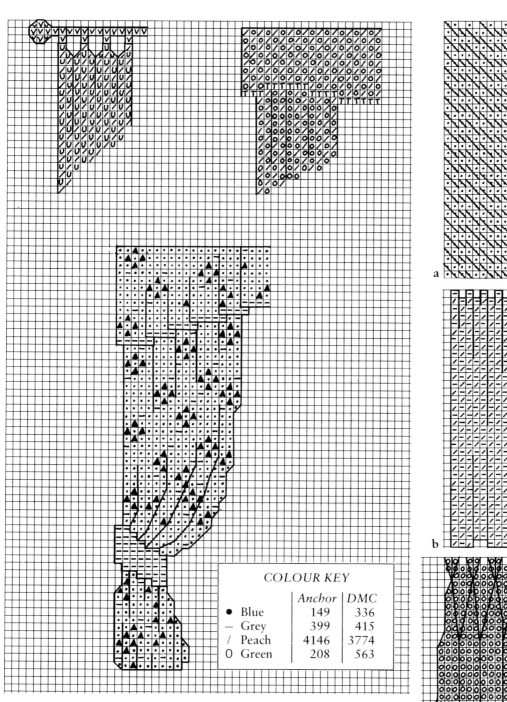

COLOUR KEY		
	Anchor	DMC
● Blue	149	336
− Grey	399	415
/ Peach	4146	3774
0 Green	208	563

CHART 30 Curtains

In examples a and c, a single colour is used for the curtain fabric. The outlines show how folds can be indicated to produce an impression of curtains hanging naturally. In b, two toning colours are used alternately. The use of outlining indicates a random folding of the fabric as it hangs.

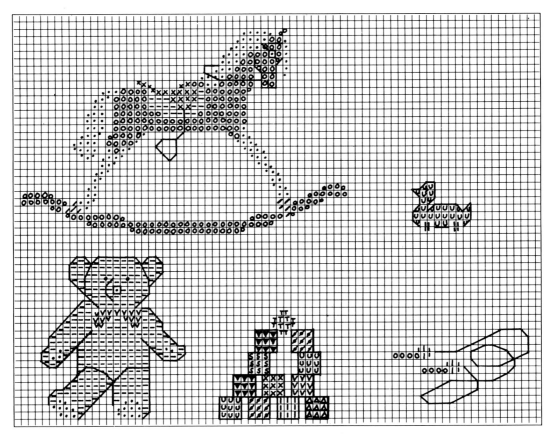

CHART 31 *Nursery items*

INSTRUCTIONS FOR NURSERY ITEMS
Follow stitch instructions for the Large Formal Garden, page 18.

COLOUR KEY
CRADLE

		Anchor	DMC
●	Pink	48	963
−	White	01	White
○	Light brown	378	407

Outlines
All outlines   Maroon (22, 814)

COLOUR KEY
TOYS

		Anchor	DMC
●	Dark Brown	381	838
○	Light brown	378	407
×	Purple	102	550
–	Gold	307	783
/	Black	403	310
S	Mauve	109	210
T	Dark blue	149	336
V	Mid blue	137	789
O	Light blue	130	799
U	Yellow	300	745
I	Red	9046	321
ø	Green	241	704
▼	Pink	76	603

Outlines

Eyes (work French knots), teddy, horse's head	Dark brown (381, 838)
Reins	Purple (102, 550)
Bricks	Dark grey (400, 317)
Skipping rope	Stone (393, 640)

Nursery items. These traditional nursery items are ideal for working in cross stitch, because of their simple lines and clear colours

THE NURSERY

Our traditional nursery toys are classics which could be found in many homes with young children.

Straight-edged shapes, such as the building blocks, are very easy to depict in cross stitch, but you can see how even curved or squashy toys can be sewn successfully in just cross stitch and outline.

The design for the cradle uses the outlining techniques described on pages 97–8 for depicting fabrics which hang in natural folds, while the angle of the back stitch stirrup swinging from the rocking horse creates life and movement.

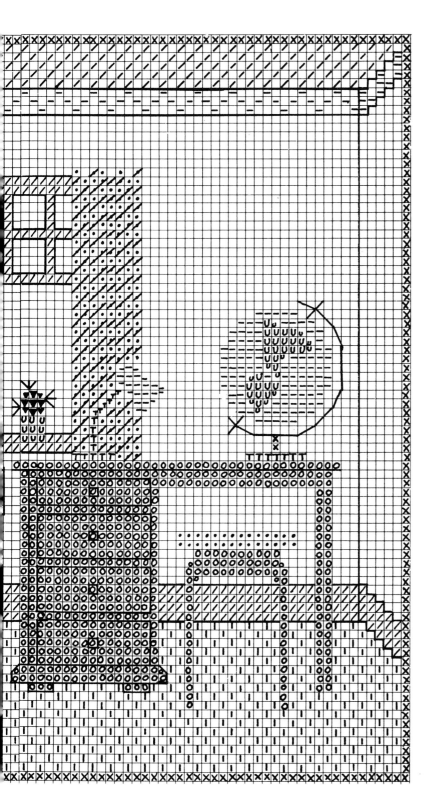

INSTRUCTIONS FOR JOHN'S BEDROOM

The design measures 120 squares by 84 squares. Follow stitch instructions for the Large Formal Garden, page 18.

COLOUR KEY

		Anchor	DMC
I	Light grey	399	415
X	Dark grey	400	317
/	White	01	White
●	Red	9046	321
O	Light brown	378	407
□	Dark brown	381	838
−	Blue	130	799
T	Black	403	310
▼	Green	244	701
∧	Yellow	300	745
U	Light brick	5975	356

Outlines

Walls, ceiling, border, skirting, books, helicopter, tennis balls, racquet strings, globe, window	Dark grey (400, 317)
Bed, table, desk, cacti	Dark brown (381, 838)
Microscope, clock hands, racquet frame, skateboard	Black (403, 310)
Clock frame	Red (9046, 321)
Curtains, pillow	White (01, white)

CHART 32
John's bedroom

John's bedroom. This teenage bedroom is worked in primary colours that give a fun, energetic feel. The bed shown in the photograph on page 98 is incorporated into the composition, but with a different headboard and quilt. To make your own design, chart items of personal significance for the teenager, as we have done here

JOHN'S BEDROOM

This cheerful young person's room in bright reds and blues is a tidy version of Barbara's son's den! The project and sports equipment have been returned neatly to their shelves and spaces and, as you can see, order reigns.

We suggested at the beginning of the chapter how you might solve the 'bed problem' by placing the bed to the side or corner of the room, and you can see this technique has been applied in our setting. The horizontal stripes of the bed cover rise and fall gently to give the impression of a soft, rounded, comfortable surface. Any small amounts of bright colours, perhaps left over in your threadbox, could be stitched into an original pattern or rainbow of stripes for a similar bedcover or throw.

John's bedroom curtains appear to have real volume and weight, due to the many little white lines which have been placed diagonally across the area of solid cross stitch. This creates the look of striped curtains which have been drawn back.

The furniture, sports equipment, books and toys are largely straight-edged, simple shapes which you can approach using the principles we have applied to the hard shapes of furniture and fittings in previous chapters. Whether photographing, sketching or just viewing the object, by approaching it straight-on and transferring it on to your graph paper at the correct scale, the most fiddly and complicated clutter can be rendered into straight lines for stitching.

Most children would be delighted to receive an image of their room and their most precious belongings – John still has his.

· 11 ·

*O*N *L*OCATION

Now that you have examined your home and its contents in such detail, you may like to widen your scope and try a design that shows your whole area.
Here we have created a picture version of an ordnance survey map. We have invented a range of symbols for all the natural features: little triangles for conifers, lollipops for the deciduous trees. We have incorporated the railway line, bridge and road, and alongside these features we have dotted in a variety of the characteristic buildings in the village.

This is a local village, and the buildings chosen are ones that mean something to us. Like many villages, it has evolved over a period of time and, as a result, has no distinct architectural style. In our embroidery the buildings represent a range from the seventeenth century to the 1930s.

The Pub and the Mill date from the 1600s, the Station and Church are Victorian, Barbara's house is Edwardian, the Village Hall is 1930s pebble dash and the Post Office and Bobby's Shop are 1930s red brick! Yet all these buildings are unified within the composition by being placed in relationship with each other and with the geography of the village. Anyone who knows the village will be able to recognise it from these few landmarks.

FROM MAP TO CHART

We started by basing our design on an ordnance survey map of the area, then en-

larged the area we wanted to stitch; we then selected just the roads we wanted to include and the railway line. We had to change the position of the railway line slightly to produce a satisfactory effect but, as you will be aware by now, we often do this (Fig 18, page 110). The railway and the roads provided an opportunity for outlining to contrast with the cross stitch worked on the rest of the map. Following the ordnance survey map, we have chosen a dotted line (worked in running stitch, Fig 17) to show footpaths and a blue line to mark the stream.

Notice that the border here has been given a rustic look by stepping a stitch out every fourth stitch. The buildings were charted

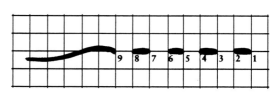

FIG 17 How to work
running stitch

CHART 33 Lettering, trees and station

INSTRUCTIONS FOR LETTERING, TREE AND STATION

Follow stitch instructions for the Large Formal Garden, page 18.

COLOUR KEY

		Anchor	DMC
/	Light stone	392	3782
0	Dark grey	400	317
●	Dark stone	393	640
X	Sandstone	373	437
+	Dark green	879	500

Outlines

Windows	White (01, White)
Tree	Dark green (879, 500)
All other outlines	Dark brown (381, 838)

from simplified sketches; as you see, they are outlined boldly in dark shades to make windows and other features stand out on such small designs. We used the original colour of the building fabric for each structure, but brightened and intensified the shade in each case to make the finished picture appear more vibrant.

However much we simplified the buildings, we wanted to ensure that they remained instantly recognisable to the occupants by retaining their overall shape and distinctive features, and this is what you should aim for too.

Do not worry too much about the comparative size of buildings. A church, for example, retains its unique features whatever its style and need not be shown larger than the houses. These are map illustrations, after all, and are therefore better shown all to a similar size.

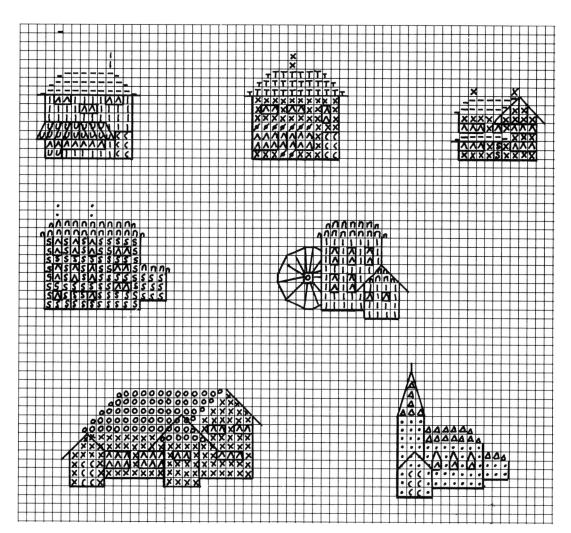

CHART 34 Village buildings

INSTRUCTIONS FOR VILLAGE BUILDINGS

Follow stitch instructions for the Large Formal Garden, page 18.

		Anchor	DMC
△	Sloe	123	791
●	Black	403	310
∩	Blue grey	922	930

COLOUR KEY

		Anchor	DMC
O	Dark grey	400	317
●	Dark stone	393	640
X	Sandstone	373	437
—	Brick	5975	356
T	Slate green	215	503
I	Pinkish brown	378	407
S	White	01	White
C	Mahogany brown	351	400
U	Maroon	22	814
∧	Light grey	399	415

Outlines

Bobby's Shop, Post Office, upper windows and side door	Black (403, 310)
Church roof	Sloe (123, 791)
Rest of Church	Dark brown (381, 838)
Gable of 'Our House'	White (01, White)
Awning of Post Office	Yellow (307, 783)
All other outlines	Dark grey (400, 317)

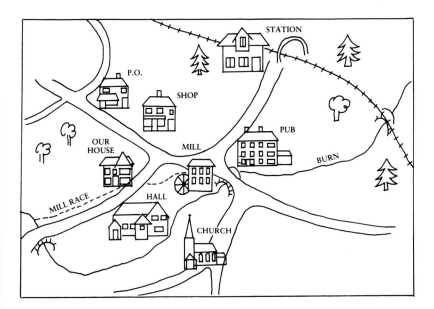

CHARTING YOUR OWN LOCALITY

FIG 18 Simplified sketch for the village map

If you are stitching your own area, it would be natural to choose just the streets around the locality in which you live and walk, as we have done. Whether it's a village, town or city, you can easily depict your 'territory'. The technique of selecting part of a detailed map, then enlarging your chosen area, narrowing down again and enlarging, as we have done, will give you the detail you need.

There were many more buildings in our immediate locality but we chose not to include them as they were of no personal significance or artistic interest. Be selective – just pick out the buildings that are significant to you.

Start by roughly drawing out the positions of the roads or paths which you want to include. Then draw in squares or rectangles for each of the buildings you would like to depict. You will probably find that some buildings overlap, whereas other areas of the map are rather empty. You can move the buildings apart, or alter the course of roads slightly to accommodate the buildings comfortably. As long as the buildings remain roughly in their relative positions, it will not be noticed if they are slightly out of place.

Village map. Although the scale of this picture makes it impossible to show the buildings in much detail, they are all still quite recognisable because we picked out distinctive features and used brighter versions of the original colours

Any other features, such as railway lines and the stream in our example, can be added next, altering their course when necessary to fit around the prominent buildings.

Use an empty corner for your title – perhaps using the name of the village, area or

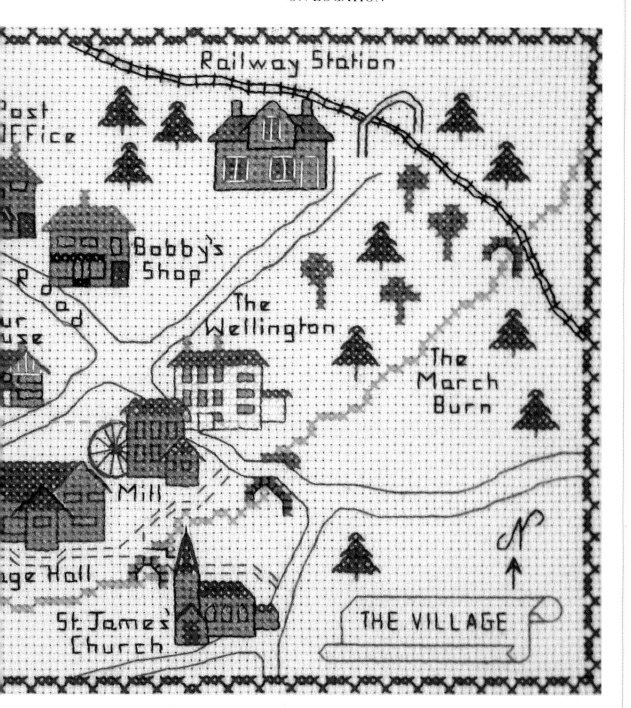

town. Other empty spaces can be filled with trees where appropriate, or perhaps a letter-box, street light or car.

12

$\mathscr{S}$IGNING $\mathscr{O}$FF

*To personalise any picture you stitch as a present or for
yourself you may wish to include your own signature or
initials, a title or date, or work in the name or the address of
the person who is to receive the gift. These charts and examples
should give you plenty of ideas for working your own
stitched lettering.*

We have relied quite heavily on the use of backstitch to enhance the cross stitch in our designs but here, in lettering, backstitch can really stand alone. The first alphabets shown here for capitals and lower case are worked entirely in backstitch and are infinitely adaptable. 'Flourishes' can be added to or taken away from capital letters for different

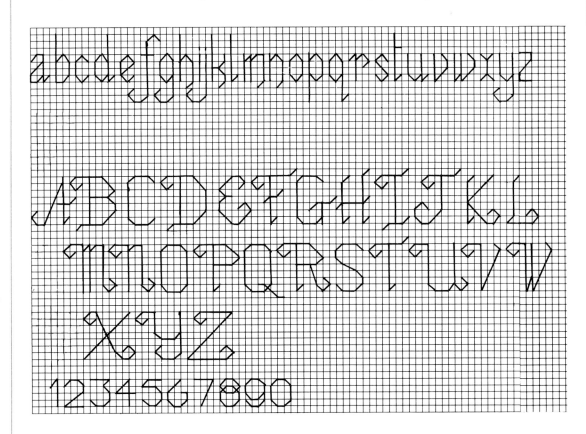

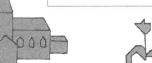

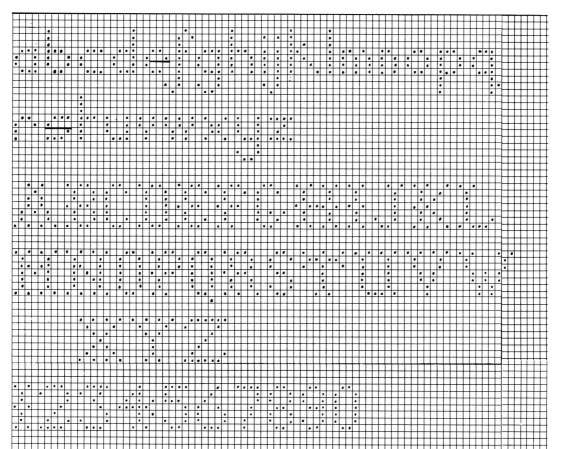

CHART 35 Alphabet and numbers
(chart does not correspond exactly with Plate)

effects, and it can be satisfying to experiment with the letters and alter them to develop antique titles or sections of lettering for your pictures. Use one or two strands of thread for light or bold effects, and try out different colours too, as these can greatly alter the appearance of words or lettering. For a more traditional look, we have also included a classic cross-stitch alphabet in lower and upper case letters.

Working a name or address on a house portrait adds that finishing touch, particularly if you include decoration, as we have done in the examples overleaf. For a birth sampler, work the name of the new baby and its date of birth, and perhaps a special personal message or blessing; for a memorial piece for someone you held dear, you may wish to stitch their name and dates into a dignified commemorative image.

Alphabets and numbers

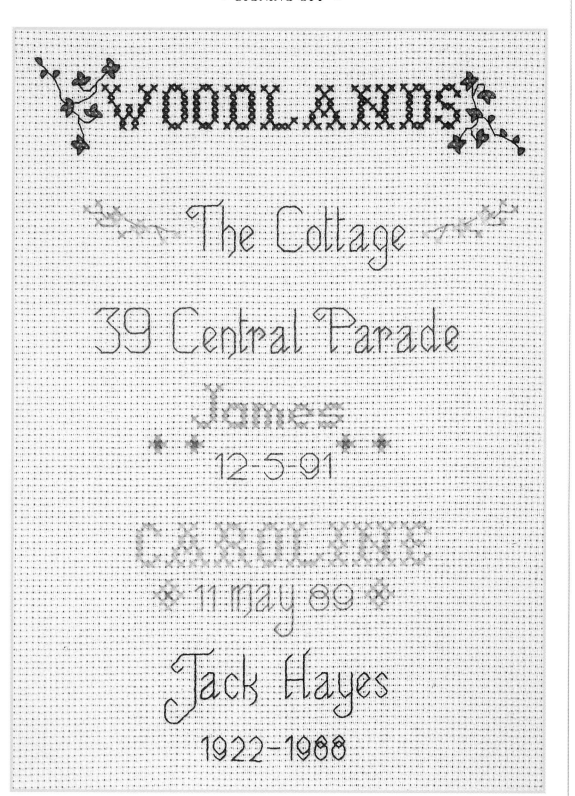

Writing styles

· 13 ·

*M*OUNTING AND *F*RAMING

The choice of a mount and frame can make or mar the presentation of your completed cross stitch picture. Here, we give basic instructions for both mounting and framing, but if you feel unsure of your ability to produce a perfect finished result then your local professional picture framer will be able to advise you on your choice and carry out the work for you.

The first step is to measure the cross stitch image, then cut a board to size measuring 1in (2.5cm) bigger all round. Fix double-sided sticky tape around the edge of the board on the reverse side. Place the fabric, image upwards, on the front of the board and stretch the material over the edges and onto the reverse side, to press against the sticky tape. Care should be taken to follow the weave of the fabric so the cross stitch image will be straight. Finally, fix masking tape over the back to ensure that the picture is securely held.

MOUNTING

Choose the colour of your mount to suit the mood of your picture, or perhaps the

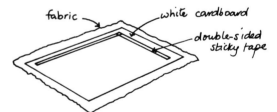

FIG 20 *Place double-sided sticky tape about 1in (2·5cm) from each edge of the card*

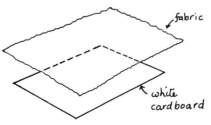

FIG 19 *Cut a board measuring 1in (2·5cm) bigger than the cross stitch image all round*

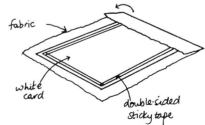

FIG 21 *Fold over each edge of the fabric in turn and secure to the sticky tape*

room in which it is to hang. Some pictures can take a double or multi-mount, and then you will have even greater freedom to co-ordinate colours. A border of 2in (5cm) is usual for an average-sized picture.

There are a range of frame shapes from which to choose, in addition to the usual rectangle. For example, an 'arch'-shaped embroidery may look best in an 'arch'-shaped mount; mounts can also be circular or oval, heart-shaped, or shaped as an initial letter. They can be given 'castle' corners or a combination of castle and plain. Our framed examples on pages 86 and 87 show how well two of the 'Cosy Corners' look in circular frames with double mounts. 'Castle corners' have been cut on one of the mounts surrounding the 'Hall' design on pages 54-5. As you will see in our framed 'Bathroom' design on page 90-1, a mount may also be chosen with a gold or silver line around the opening edge to reflect the gold or silver of the frame – and, in this case, the gold of the taps in our cross stitch design. Alternatively, a groove can be cut in the mount to make a white line as an edging.

With needlework one can use lace or ribbon to great effect. Bows look attractive on a contrasting mountboard, while furnishing material or velvet can be used to cover the mountboard if you wish to co-ordinate with decor. An experienced framer will be familiar with all these techniques and styles, and will be happy to suggest others if this is something you would rather not tackle yourself.

As far as the finished result is concerned, the choice of mount is more important than the choice of frame: it has a bigger impact, covers more area, and can make or destroy a picture.

FRAMING

With mounted pictures the frame must suit both the image and the mount; usually only a narrow frame is needed. There are thousands of different mouldings in modern and traditional styles, colours and materials: antiqued gilts and silvers, woods, laminates, lacquers and aluminium mouldings are possible choices for needlecraft.

Unmounted pictures generally look better in a heavier frame. Miniature needleworks, that is up to 5in (12.5cm) square, look particularly good in a heavy frame 2-3in (5-7.5cm) wide. Old samplers and tapestries lend themselves to old maple or stained oak frames, sometimes with a gold slip inserted in the 'rebate', where the moulding meets the picture or mount; this is how they were framed in Victorian times.

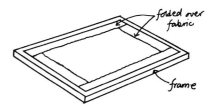

FIG 22 *If using a ready-made frame, place the mounted embroidery carefully into it and secure firmly in place by replacing the frame backing card*

To make a frame the picture with mount is measured and the moulding mitred to the size. It is joined then on an 'underpinner,' which is a modern invention, which joins without anything being visible from top and sides. Glass is cut to the frame and fitted in with a hardboard back, and masking taped around the edge to prevent dust finding its way under the glass.

MATERIALS, KITS AND SUPPLIERS

Throughout the book we have used quite simple everyday tools: pencils, rubbers, rulers, scissors and sticky tape. In addition, a camera and a file of inspiring pictures from magazines and brochures are invaluable.

For the Aida and Linda fabrics we have mentioned, we recommend you seek out a good needlecraft shop or centre in your area, which appear in directories under 'Art Embroidery' or 'Craft Retailers'. Any specialist embroidery retailer will stock many sizes and colours of evenweave fabric, and probably more than one range of stranded cottons.

The transparent graph paper we have become used to using is now more readily available. If your embroidery centre does not have a supply, try an artist's materials shop or quality stationer's.

Barbara Thompson Designs produce a range of counted-thread cross stitch kits which are widely available. Write to Ann Green at 18 Rumbold Road, Edgerton, Huddersfield, West Yorkshire, HD3 3DB, for a colour brochure and stockists list.

Designs featured in this book which are also available as kits:
The Large Formal Garden
Grey Fireplace Drawing Room
John's Bedroom
Hall with Chaise-longue
The Green Bathroom (kit available in blue colourway only)
The Yellow and Gold Kitchen
The Spiky Top Conservatory
The Mahogany Conservatory

INTERNATIONAL OUTLETS FOR BARBARA THOMPSON DESIGNS
France
Ouvrage, 69 Rue St. Martin, 75004 Paris
Angele Gaspard & Cie, 65 Rue Pierre Demours, 75017 Paris
Blue de Chine, 23 Rue Marsoulan, 75012 Paris
Dolet Doll's House, 12 Rue Louis Roguet, 45000 Orleans

Italy
Sybilla, Via Nannetti 1, 40069 Zola Predosa, Bologna
Divina S.R.L., Piazza San't Ambrogio, 8, 20123 Milano
Biondetti, Fontane Via Alessandre Volta 12/a 31050 Villorba

Spain
Bimbi, 49 Hermosilla, 28001 Madrid
Donna, Provencia 256, 08008 Barcelona
Petit Punt, Muntaner 428, Tienda 6, 08006 Barcelona
Tricot, Avg Conqueridor, 89 bis, 07760 Ciudaella a de Menorca, Baleares

New Zealand
Broomfields, Merivale Mall, Christchurch, PO Box 21205

Canada
Patricia Ann's Needlecraft, 870 C 13 Ave, Campbell River, British Columbia V9W 4H2

$\mathscr{A}$CKNOWLEDGEMENTS

We wish to acknowledge the help given by the following friends and relatives:

Edith Hayes, Jenny Mathers, Rita Arcarnley, Kathy Taylor, Anna Bajerski, Janelle Allison, Chrissie Rosby, Colin Sherrington, Sue Chapman, Ian Thompson and Roy Green.

We are also grateful to Janelle Allison, Edith Hayes and Wendy Stephenson, who have allowed us to publish photographs of their 'house portraits'.

Finally, we would like to thank Pam Ward at Huddersfield Picture Framing Company for her wonderfully sympathetic framing of our work, and Jonathan Bosley (pages 50/51, 79), Di Lewis (pages 2, 6, 54/55, 66/67, 70/71, 90), and John Woods at John Woods Photography, Huddersfield (pages 14, 18/19, 26, 27, 30, 38, 42, 78, 82, 86, 87, 91, 95, 98, 99, 103, 111, 114, 115), for their expert photographs of our finished designs.

INDEX

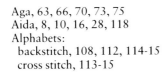

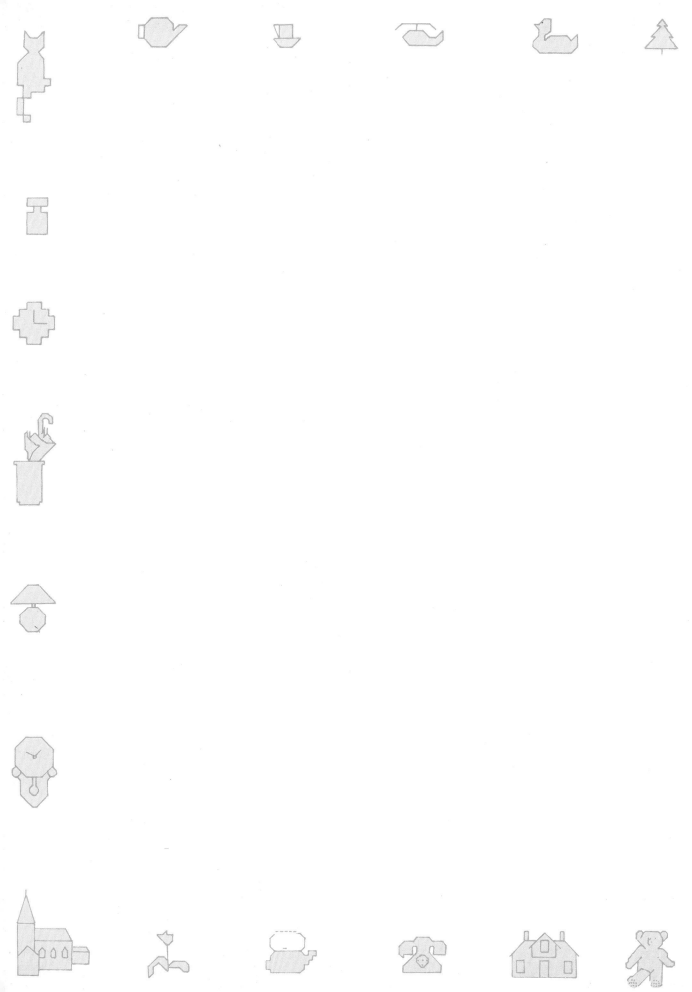